WHAT OTHERS ARE SAYING ABOUT
DON'T OWN DON'T RENT LIVE WELL

"There are two basic ways to achieve financial freedom: increase our income or decrease our expenses. A lot of books try to show us how to make more money but this book provides us with an innovative strategy for eliminating our biggest monthly expense. We all need a place to stay. What if we could stay for free?"

—David Rendall, Speaker, Trainer and Author of
The Freak Factor: Discovering Uniqueness by Flaunting Weakness

"Why buy a house and be enslaved to debt, when you can live debt-free and save money? This is a brilliant concept that is realistic and doable!"

—Elizabeth McMillion, Stay-At-Home Mom & Small Business Owner

"Shared with quirky wit, the tale of Matthew and Fiona's journey into, around, and out from under a Mountain of Debt. Here is a credible escape route with techniques YOU can use to conquer debt and live your life well."

—Art Noll, Ocean Kayak Guide / Vagabond

"Matthew and Fiona have led the way by example in resetting their thinking and redesigning a purposeful and fulfilling lifestyle. Their liberating insight came by fluke causing them to find the formulas and systematize every procedure for easy replication at any property, by anyone. They also had the genius to redefine the terms of their roles in a way that commands respect and delivers more value for everyone involved. Debt-free and living life on your own terms - who wouldn't want that?"

—**Donna Kim Brand**, GlobaLearningNetwork.com

"A fluid, compelling narrative about a fun, mobile, and comfortable lifestyle that affords readers the opportunity to pursue their passions. The Community Executive may well become the iconic profession for the 21st century."

—**Eric G. Olive**, EgoWebInteractive.com

"As a now retired financial planner, I sure wish I had known this stuff. I could've helped my clients so much more."

—**Jim Richardson**, Executive Producer of the Power of 10 Event

"Simply Profound! What they teach brings *Freedom* back to the American Dream. I could easily see this trigger a revolution in the real estate and financial world!"

—**Keith Gilmore**, Marketing Consultant, Husband and Father of Two

"It was always engrained in me that if you didn't own a home, you would always be "poor" and never own anything. I couldn't have been more wrong. With a little discipline, not owning can actually give you more money in your pocket, leave you with less responsibility and a lot less headache."

—**Troy Bystol**, Entrepreneur

"Finally, a practical way to break away from the rat race that doesn't involve the financial risks of starting a business. This book motivated my wife and me to break away from the standard housing dilemma and pursue our dreams of travel and homeschooling our daughter."

—**Dave Gennrich**, Mechanical Engineer

"Many people dream of living in exotic, far-away places, yet get discouraged or give up on the dream because of the challenges of finding a home and a job. The Peters bridge the gap from dream to reality with their creative and innovative solution to financing the life one chooses. Their book guides people step-by-step, streamlining the process, and enjoying the financial freedom that such a life brings. I highly recommend this book."

—**Cara B. Goodman**, Entrepreneur & "Recovering Attorney"

"Matthew and Fiona are on to something very powerful here. In this book awaits practical hope to those struggling financially by providing the tools that will empower them to take back control and live life on their own terms!"

—**Cort Howard,** Broker-Owner, Howard and Williams

"To be honest, I was expecting yet another fluffy "go after your dreams" type book. And, while there is an inspirational side, there is also a very practical "how-to" side from which anyone truly wanting to manage their finances more wisely and live life a bit more "free" could benefit. The question is, how free do you want to be?"

—**John Pollard**, Musician & Technology Evangelist

"I found the chapters informative, concise and entertaining. Weaving their personal journey into the professional content makes for an easy read with well timed reliefs."

—**Itay T. Klaz, MD**

"Matthew's unique system for creating a lifestyle of freedom and reduced stress is brilliant. This is a must-read for anyone who is looking to save money and not be tied down by bills."

—**Dustin Maher**, America's Trainer to the Moms, www.DustinMaherFitness.com

"This book is intriguing, inspirational and accessible. They share the knowledge and the tools necessary to powerfully and purposefully take our financial future in a new and achievable direction towards prosperity."

—**Diane G. Peters**, Lecturer & Entrepreneur

"This book represents a truly progressive approach; a new way of thinking and living that may make reaching your family and financial goals (like debt-freedom) more practical and achievable - especially in a down economy. Save yourself years of interest payments while freeing yourself up to follow your passions. They teach from experience - even making it fun. I have known Matthew & Fiona for almost 20 years and I'm always impressed by their character and integrity."

—**Rion Freeberg**, Entrepreneur & World Traveler
www.RionFreeberg.com

"I am pragmatist and an entrepreneur and I shy away from unproven ideas. These ideas are my favorite meal because the recipes have been tried and proven."

—**Dr. Tom Collins**

"An honest, no-nonsense guide to getting out from under the mountain of debt that most of America is trapped under. Their personal and sincere stories are both entertaining and educational. They've been able to simplify something that can seem so scary into something manageable."

—**Josh P.**, Actor & Commercial Director

Don't Own Don't Rent Live Well

How to be DEBT FREE
Build Your Nest Egg &
Live Life on Your Own Terms

MATTHEW PETERS
FIONA PETERS

NEW YORK

Don't Own Don't Rent Live Well

How to be DEBT FREE *Build Your Nest Egg & Live Life on Your Own Terms*

by MATTHEW PETERS, FIONA PETERS

ISBN 978-1-60037-880-5 (paperback)

ISBN 978-1-60037-881-2 (epub)

Library of Congress Control Number: 2010939063

Published by:

MORGAN JAMES PUBLISHING
The Entrepreneurial Publisher
5 Penn Plaza, 23rd Floor
New York City, New York 10001
(212) 655-5470 Office
(516) 908-4496 Fax
www.MorganJamesPublishing.com

Cover Design by:
Rachel Lopez
rachel@r2cdesign.com

Interior Design by:
Bonnie Bushman
bbushman@bresnan.net

In an effort to support local communities, raise awareness and funds, Morgan James Publishing donates one percent of all book sales for the life of each book to Habitat for Humanity.

Get involved today, visit
www.HelpHabitatForHumanity.org.

Dedicated to our children, Aidian and Kaiya

May you never be too intimidated to live your dreams.

ACKNOWLEDGMENTS

No one ever accomplishes any major project on their own. It is only through words of encouragement, constructive criticism and emotional support that this book has made it to your hands.

Though this book is written by me in the first person, my wife, Fiona, has encouraged and supported me above everyone else. She is the other half of my life; this story is *our story*. Each discovery and lesson taught here is our joint creation.

I'd like to say thank you to my parents, Jim and Diane Peters, for believing in me through every step of this journey. I owe a debt of gratitude for their lasting encouragement and for fostering in me the entrepreneurial spirit at a very early age.

To Erlinda and Charlie Reyes, for their generosity and support and for being engaged in the lives of our children.

To Vince and Mary Arts, for giving Fiona and me the opportunity to test and build this system.

To Michelle Hegg and Steve Householder, for their support over the last six years. They are an integral part in making our amazing lifestyle possible.

To Richard McKenzie, for his ongoing generosity and encouragement.

To Keith Gilmore for his friendship, sense of humor and words of wisdom.

To Cort Howard for his unique perspective into an industry I am continuously learning about.

To David Gennrich, Trent Schaller, Diane Peters, Troy Bystol, Alicia Butz, Kelly, Art Noll, Eric Olive, Eric Herkert-Oakland and Peggy Kruse, for their diverse perspectives and insight into how to make this book better for the reader.

To Josh Wimmer, for his outstanding job editing this book.

CONTENTS

NOTE

Ah...money. Some people say it isn't important. But like Les Brown, I have always believed it ranked up there with oxygen. I need it to live. I want a nice place to come home to, a luxury car to drive, a secure, debt-free future and a big flat-screen for my kids to watch the same episode of *Dora the Explorer* on over and over again. And those people who tell me that money isn't important to them? I bet they're lying.

In a time when 15 million Americans are out of work, struggling to get out of debt, and one in four houses are underwater with their mortgage, how do we make more money? Isn't that the real question?

Here's a solution: Just keep more of it! Housing is your biggest expense, even before income taxes. According the Department of Labor, based on an average income of $63,091, taxes equal 21 percent of your expenses. Housing surpasses that, by constituting an unbelievable *34 percent* of expenses! That's $16,920 a year of your *after-tax* dollars. How would you like a $16,920 annual raise?

You can have it. Imagine living in a luxury 3-bedroom, 2-bathroom town house with an attached garage and private fenced-in yard ALL FOR FREE. That's what Matthew and I do. Instead of paying rent or a mortgage, we can spend our money elsewhere. That $16,920 goes into *our* pocket instead of a lender's or a landlord's.

This book is about our system—how we did it and how you can, too. It's about eliminating your highest monthly expenses and keeping that money in your pocket. And best of all, anyone can do it!

And about that flat-panel TV: I already regret buying a 32-inch model. What was I thinking? I practically have to squint to see Boots.

Fiona Peters
Property Manager & Entrepreneur

PREFACE

As I step out of the car, the chill of the crisp night air hits my face. It's Tuesday, December 15, and I heard we could have a low of 16 degrees tonight. My wife, Fiona, and I enter one of the nicest restaurants in the city fashionably late. Wall sconces dimly light the place. Classy piano music plays over the murmur of a hundred conversations. The air is rich with the aroma of steak, and glasses full of fine wine clink all around us.

As the host leads us toward the back of the restaurant, we pass several groups of smiling people entrenched in conversation. As we approach our party, tucked behind chocolate-colored velvet curtains, Susan spots us and announces our arrival. Our friends and coworkers greet us with open arms and smile. "They're here!"

We are seated, and the server asks if we would like something to drink. I have never had a martini before, and I know that this place is known for theirs. When it arrives, I'm drawn to it as if there were some sort of magnet on the rim. Mmm…equally fruity and dry. Next, I order a 22-ounce porterhouse steak. When our host for the evening says, "Get whatever you like," he means it. Wow, this is the high life!

Every year the family we work with puts on a little get-together at a fabulous restaurant. There's always great conversation, hilarious stories about crazy clients, amazing food, spirits and, of course, the infamous white-elephant gift exchange. This year we lucked out and got a pink Snuggie.

As I sit back, savoring my martini, I look over the table, half-listening to the chatter and laughter. My mind drifts, and then time freezes and conversations blur as I realize just how special this night is. I go through dinner in a half-daze thinking that it's some kind of surreal dream.

As Fiona and I walk away from the restaurant later, I realize that we have it all. We went out for a fancy dinner, and it didn't cost us a dime.

We have it really good. Choosing the life direction that we have for the last nine years has been one of the best decisions we've ever made.

I remember all the times we were asked, "So, what do you do?" As the years passed, I would respond with, "I'm an audiovisual tech at the university and a resident manager." Then: "I own a multimedia company, and I am a resident manager." Later: "I'm a songwriter, filmmaker and a resident manager."

People always ask more questions about being a resident manager than anything else. And through the course of such conversations, our friends discover that Fiona and I…

- Pay absolutely nothing for our personal housing—and haven't in many, many years
- Own three houses and don't live in any of them
- Vacation all over the world *and pay for our travels in cash*
- Own 137 acres on a lake in another country—*paid for*
- Are in the process of remodeling our lake house
- Have the ability to follow our dreams
- Spend as much time with our children and together as a couple as we choose
- Have the freedom to set our own schedule

Our friends know we have something special, but only recently have I fully realized it myself. I pretty much took what we have for granted.

A few years back, Fiona and I figured out a way to have it all—time, possessions, the chance to travel, and the ability to pay off all of our debts and build our nest egg.

In trade for spending an average of four hours per month managing a property, we receive a **free** 1,400-square-foot, 3-bedroom, 2-bathroom town house apartment with a fenced-in backyard and attached garage. We live a block from a beach in one of the best places to live on earth.[1] We don't pay rent, mortgage or property taxes anymore; we pay *no* condo fees, and many of our utilities are free, too.

We have full use of any of three resort-quality clubhouses, swimming pools, gyms and meeting rooms, too. Most important of all, we are blessed with the support of a great management company and a full maintenance team, including 24-hour emergency coverage.

Over the years Fiona and I have learned the hard way—not by taking classes or reading books on how to manage real estate. (We didn't do that until years later.) From our struggles, we have created a system that works amazingly well. We've shared how we do it with a couple of people, but for the most part we've kept this little secret to ourselves. Until now.

I want to take you on a journey. I'm about to show you how we came to this amazing place in our lives. To talk about what *we* have is one thing, but to show *you* how to achieve your financial goals and other aspirations is another thing entirely. In the following pages I will lay out a step-by-step guide to how you can have what we have, or even more.

But first, I want to tell you just how we fell into our situation, because when Fiona and I started our life together, we never thought of being resident managers or property managers, or of owning rental property ourselves.

Mathew Peters

---

1 *Money*, "Best Places to Live": http://money.cnn.com/magazines/moneymag/bplive/2007/index.html

THE
BEGINNING

Chapter 1

OUR STORY:
IF WE CAN DO IT,
SO CAN YOU

It had been almost a year since my college graduation. I was living in the basement of my parents' child-care center and trying to make my multilevel marketing distributorship pay off. I was showing people how they could save money on household goods by becoming a distributor and buying through themselves.

During the day, I worked at a local T-shirt distribution center picking shirts for orders and placing them into boxes to be weighed before shipping. I was terrible at it; I had zero passion for it. My mind would wander so much that I would often get off count or be told to speed up. To alleviate the monotony, I would count in English, and then in Spanish and Korean. One day, I was called into my supervisor's office. He said that I was slow and inefficient, and he warned me to shape up or ship out!

I started to hate working there. I liked most of the people I worked with, but after a while I began to wonder why they stayed. One woman I worked with had been picking and packing shirts for more than 15 years. I had a problem with it before 15 days!

I got called into my supervisor's office again. This time it looked like I was about to get the axe, so I said to him, "I'm not happy here, and this isn't a good fit for me. I appreciate the job, but I think it is time for me to move on." He and I finally agreed on something.

When I checked the mail, I would see letters from Chase Bank, Discover, Wells Fargo, Marathon Oil and at least three other creditors several times a week. I had nearly maxed out *seven credit cards*. The cards allowed me to do so many things—to go on trips, buy tires for my car, fix my car, buy gas for my car, get groceries. They had become open accounts for anything and everything.

Many of the bills would just sit on my kitchen counter for weeks, unopened. I had no money coming in, so I just let them pile up. Out of sight, out of mind. Messages from collectors filled my answering machine, and I learned not to answer the phone anymore. Those creditors were the first people to ever call me "Mr. Peters."

From time to time, I would satisfy the thirstiest of them with a payment using one of the paper checks another credit card provided for me. I didn't know that I was paying a higher interest rate when I used those checks. It was a very bad situation, to say the least. Fortunately, my basement lodgings didn't cost me anything, and my car had been a college gift from my parents.

Yep, I felt like a real winner. I had graduated college, and this is how I was using my education. I was determined to improve my situation.

My girlfriend, Fiona, and I continued to run our multilevel marketing business by spending hours upon hours drumming up new accounts. Though I lost a lot of money on that venture, it did stretch me in a good way, teaching me to be more outgoing and getting me out of my shell. I would give sales presentations to groups of three to ten people up to 100 miles away. Of course, since we were traveling all over the Midwest, we were racking up thousands of miles on my failing car.

On a sunny afternoon, we were "dream building" by browsing past a car lot when a friendly salesman approached. I wasn't even shopping for a car, but he talked me into a test-drive. The next thing you know, Fiona and I were in his office. He was very good at what he did.

We were pleasantly surprised to learn that we qualified for a car loan. The friendly salesman suggested that I get the extended service plan and life insurance policy to be *completely* covered. It was not until later that I realized that I had not only paid full sticker price for the car, but was also financing *all* of the up-sells at a whopping 15.9 percent interest rate, too. Yes, I know: *What a sucker!* I can't believe I agreed to all of that either.

Fiona and I agreed that we were on the wrong track financially. We were broke and buried in credit card debt with nothing to show for it. Now we had added to that burden a car with 85,000 miles, worth 70 percent of what we had paid for it. And when we got married, my bad credit became her bad credit. Together, we had accrued over $38,000 in consumer credit debt.

We took a week long honeymoon in northern Wisconsin and Upper Michigan, staying in lighthouses and bed-and-breakfasts. One night, we were awoken by our host at 1 a.m. to gather around the top of the light tower to watch an incredible Northern Lights display for about an hour. The whole experience was magical.

On that trip, we caught the travel bug and knew we wanted to see more of the world and enjoy more freedom to go where we wanted to, when we wanted to. We realized that no matter what jobs we held, we were *not* nine-to-fivers!

During our honeymoon we realized that our multilevel marketing business was actually keeping us *away* from our goals instead of bringing us closer to them. So we broke off our ties with it, stopped paying dues and never looked back.

We dreaded returning to our day jobs. I was working part-time at Eddie Bauer, where I cheerfully folded shirt after shirt, following those customers who wanted to see what every shirt looked like unfolded. (Hey, just look at the mannequin, pal!) I was also on the morning team at Best Buy stocking heavy tube TVs, and pallets of radios, telephones, computers and other electronics every morning at five thirty. After two weeks, I was made a senior customer service representative. It was my first promotion.

When I became a senior rep, I got paid more, but exchanged my backaches for headaches. It was mandatory to work weekends and strange shifts—e.g., to close one night and then open the next day. It wasn't a career track I wanted to be on.

A few months later, Fiona and I quit our jobs (another well-calculated move!). We realized that we only lived in Wisconsin because that was where our families were. I was known locally as "Jim and Diane's son," and after a while, I wanted to be known for being *me*. We wanted our own identity as a couple, and to prove we could make it on our own.

Heading Out On Our Own

We gave notice to end our apartment lease, packed up all of our belongings and stuffed them into a mini warehouse. We took the money we had received as wedding gifts and decided to head west without any reservations. We got in our overpriced, 15.9 percent APR used car and left for what we call to this day our "extended honeymoon." We were fascinated with the western states and were secretly looking for a new place to call home.

Traveling out there was the time of our lives. We felt completely liberated. We cut across the plains states and stopped in Wall, South Dakota. We toured Wall Drug and headed to the Badlands and the Black Hills. Once, we stayed in a tent in Custer State Park, where two buffalos fought about 10 feet from us. We headed up to Devil's Tower and then north into Montana, where I drove the then–speed limit—a "reasonable and prudent" 110 mph. It was fun, but a little scary in our sedan.

We hiked through bear country in Glacier National Park, staying at St. Mary's campground, where we heard elk bugling in the distance while we lay awake, staring up at the big Montana sky. One night it started to snow, and it became too cold for us to sleep in out $30 Wal-Mart tent.

I remember looking for a motel for over an hour. My two criteria were that it couldn't cost more than $40 a night, and that we didn't see any cockroaches. I wanted an inexpensive room first because I was a cheapskate about some things, and second because we wanted to delay our return to reality. The faster we spent our money, the sooner we would have to head back home.

From there we rocketed down to Arizona. It was in sunny Scottsdale that we chose to relocate.

When we applied for an apartment there, the manager said our credit was so bad that we needed a co-signer. I called my parents from the manager's office, confident that they would help us—but they said no. They reminded me that I wanted more independence and to prove I could be on my own.

We then called Fiona's parents, and they said no as well. I have to say, looking back on it now, it was probably the best thing our parents could have done for us. They realized we were two educated adults, now married, and that we needed to test our independence. Plus, they saved me the emasculation of going to my parents to bail me out of the credit mess I had created. Having any of them co-sign would have deprived me of that lesson, as well as some of our dignity as a couple.

But try recovering from being turned down by both set of parents in front of a property manager! The manager made a phone call and, after some deliberation, she finally said that if we could give them a double security deposit (the equivalent of two months of rent), we could sign a lease. Looking back, I can only imagine how desperate they were for renters. We had no jobs, bad credit and no savings!

When we returned to Wisconsin to gather our belongings, my parents lent us $2,100 to cover our moving expenses. Then we loaded up our 24-foot Ryder truck, hitched up our car and headed out to Arizona for a fresh start.

Within a month, Fiona landed a great job with Del Webb. I took temporary jobs. One stint had me working for BF Goodrich testing the inflatable emergency slides that pop out of passenger airplanes.

Aeronautical researchers would stand us up front to back, packed tightly in a line at the door of a mock fuselage. When a bell rang, we exited the plane in a peaceful and orderly fashion—neatly stacked front to back, just like in a real-life scenario.

Then they tested the slide's buoyancy by squishing all 60 of us onto the slide while it floated in a 3-foot-deep swimming pool of cold water. After about 15 minutes, they began to let the air out of the center chamber to see how much we could endure without mentally flipping out. Fortunately, a few weeks after moving, I started a position as an audiovisual tech at a local resort.

Fiona was proactive enough to take steps toward getting us connected with a reputable credit consolidation service. They brought all of our credit card interest down to 0 percent (some cards were at 21 percent) and were able to negotiate down some of our other debt for us, too. The catch was that we had to make every single $500 monthly payment or we would immediately forfeit the deal, and all our interest would be reinstated.

With our rent at $1,000 a month, Fiona and I quickly realized our housing expense was taking a huge bite out of our tiny income. We chose not to have a phone, because the phone company wanted a $200 deposit due to our terrible credit. We had a TV, but no signal or cable, so it just sat quietly in the corner. No Internet or cell phone, either. What we did have was voicemail. We used the pay phone outside a Burger King across the street to check it and returned calls using a calling card.

During that time, we concentrated on paying off our debt and strengthening our marriage. One of our saving graces was a discount grocery store across the street, where we were able to buy inexpensive groceries. One fond memory is the especially tasty boxes of mac-and-cheese we found on special for 25 cents a box when they were purchased by the case. Early on, most of our meals started box-bound in dry or powder form; they rarely cost more than $2 total for the two of us. I remember one day scraping together money to buy groceries and seeing that the woman in front of us in the checkout line was buying steak, chicken and fruit with food stamps. I was so jealous.

At my job at the resort, chafing dishes holding catering leftovers were brought into the back hallways after the banquet halls were cleared. I would fill pie tins with the leftovers and take them home. Another bonus was that I received one or two meals per day in the resort cafeteria. Sometimes I came into work an hour early just to get another free meal.

After being so extravagant and putting everything on credit cards over the previous three years, we had become extremely frugal—no frills, no entertainment, no extra anything. It was pretty much rent, food, gas, insurance, voicemail and debt repayment. As financial teacher and radio talk show host Dave Ramsey says: "You got to be on beans and rice, rice and beans."

How a Housing U-Turn Led to Financial Freedom

One morning Fiona saw a sign in the clubhouse at our apartment complex that said they were looking for weekend help. The job required that someone answer phones, show the model apartment and bake cookies for those who stopped in to see our 218-unit complex. She applied and began working there four hours a day on both Saturdays and Sundays.

It was a quiet job, with very little foot traffic and few phone calls. Sometimes I would go in and hang out with her, and eat a few Otis Spunkmeyer cookies as they came out of the warming oven. Often, she would read a book, use the Internet, work on our finances or catch up on other work while she was at her post.

In return for occupying the office, the management company paid her about $10 an hour *and* subtracted $400 a month from our rent. That meant that for sitting at a desk and answering phones—basically, *being a warm body*—she was getting paid the equivalent of $22.50 an hour. We were now paying $600 per month for a luxury apartment that all our fellow renters were paying $1,000 or more for and were making another $240 a month, just for some weekend help.

Almost everyone pays for their housing with money they keep after income taxes have been taken out. Taxes alone can diminish your spending power 28%-40%.

We quickly realized that the $400 off of our rent actually went much further than $400 income from a "normal" job would have. Because the money was taken directly from our rent, there were no taxes taken out. And the fact is that almost everyone pays for their housing with money they keep *after* income taxes have been taken out. Taxes alone can diminish your spending power by 28 to 40 percent.

This is why reduced rent is more valuable than gross employee pay for the same amount. If you can wrap your brain around this, you will begin to see how powerful this concept can be when it comes to giving you the freedom to do what you please.

It wasn't long before we were able to squirrel away some money. Our debt payment was now a consistent $500 a month, and we had just dropped our monthly expenses by roughly $700. Any extra money we had was applied to our debt, to pay it off more quickly. And Fiona and I had already moved over to an all-cash system due to our lack of available credit.

This opportunity proved to be a turning point for us financially. We realized that there were ways of living other than those we had been brought up hearing about. Though we still wanted to own a house someday, the idea that we could live for a fraction of the cost of everyone else around us simply by working a few hours a week really appealed.

Almost a year had passed when I received a call from my mother. She said that Mary, an acquaintance of hers, had mentioned that a job was opening at the University of Wisconsin that I might qualify for. I knew it was a long shot for me to get a good government job at this point in my career, but I applied for it just the same.

I talked to Fiona about moving back to Wisconsin, and she was hesitant—returning to cold, harsh winters was unappealing—but open to it. After setting up a job interview for early the following month, we decided to sell half of everything we owned to cover our moving expenses.

Moving Back

Once again, we packed up a moving truck, but this time headed east. We moved into my parents' house for a few weeks while we looked for housing and employment. Fiona was checking the newspaper for job openings when she found an ad for a resident manager position at a college rooming house. We thought we could possibly use her experience working weekends at the clubhouse in Arizona to get the position.

Fiona was able to schedule an interview with the owners. A couple days later, we met with them at their private residence. Vince and Mary greeted us with smiles and welcomed us in. About a minute into our casual interview, Vince said to Mary, "I think they'll do fine." Mary was a little more hesitant and continued to ask more questions. They told us that the chosen couple would be responsible for answering questions via phone, advertising the rooms they had for rent, showing the rooms, collecting rent, filling out leases, conflict resolution, shoveling snow off the walk, mowing the 3- by 12-foot lawn and some light maintenance. In return, they were offering us a 2-bedroom apartment, a parking space (a huge bonus since the rooming house was downtown), free phone, free electricity and free heat. It sounded like a great deal to me.

The Cochrane House was a 17-unit "rooming house" on UW-Madison's fraternity and sorority row. The busyness and noise would be a change from the quiet atmosphere of the small town where my parents lived.

The house was for women only. Almost all of them were students or grad students at UW. Each of them had a separate bedroom, but shared bathrooms, a huge commercial kitchen, a dining area and a lounge.

Fiona and I mentioned that we both had full-time jobs and that we wouldn't be able to be in the house 24/7. After discussing Vince and Mary's most important concerns, we agreed upon an arrangement in which I would just keep a pager with me. And after about 20 more minutes, Vince and Mary looked at each other and agreed that we would be right for the position. That was the start of our second position managing rental property.

My biggest concern with the position was the maintenance. I had done a little construction work in the past, had taken wood shop in high school, had learned a few things from my father and grandfather and could read a tape measure. In the end, I just figured it out as I went. I ended up doing little things like unclogging drains, turning off running toilets and catching bats in the upstairs hallway.

At the interview we agreed that if I felt that a maintenance task was beyond my fairly limited abilities, I'd call a local contractor from Vince and Mary's preapproved contractor list. This was a huge weight off my shoulders. I was not responsible for fixing everything that broke in the 130-year-old house!

I did get the university position we had moved to Wisconsin for. While working full-time, I kept a pager on my belt in the case of a maintenance emergency at the house. Fortunately, I was only a 15-minute bike ride away. And during the three years we were there, I only had to run to the house twice.

Our Great Escape

We were resident managers for about five months, and everything was in full swing. The house was 100 percent occupied for the season, and things began to quiet down right before Christmas. I had been working for UW for about four months when we decided to use up all of my vacation time in one shot and travel through Argentina for five weeks.

We had saved about $10,000 cash in the bank over the past several months, and we figured our trip would take about $7,000 to do it right. I talked to my supervisor at work, and he said I could go as long as I tied up any loose ends before I left. However, Vince and Mary were not as supportive as he was. We assured them that we had very capable, professional and trustworthy friends watching over the house while we were away.

Before deciding to go on our trip and buying airline tickets, we found a couple we knew we could trust to tend to our duties. We explained everything to them, gave them contact numbers and procedures and a list of basic duties, and paid them $100 a week to do it. We planned our trip during the slowest time of the year so that it would be a cakewalk for them.

Off we went to beautiful Buenos Aires for a week, followed by backpacking across the plains of Patagonia and journey through the temperate rain forests of bamboo, over mountain passes, across rivers while knee-deep in glacial melt and across glaciers in Tierra del Fuego. We ended up south of the city of Ushuaia on a sailboat in the Beagle Channel watching penguins and sea lions. It was an amazing five weeks, just for the two of us.

While we were gone, we checked in with our friends twice. We had voicemail and email through which they could contact us if necessary, but they never had to. When we returned, everything was fine. We found out that the fire department had showed up, due to a call about a smoky smell, but there hadn't been any real problem. And even if there had been a real emergency, our replacements would have worked it all out like the capable adults they were.

Upon our return, we started showing units to students for the following school year for August move-ins. That was mid-January. Soon, we were fully rented again for the next term. We pushed to get the house rented quickly so that we wouldn't have to think about it anymore. Slowly but surely, we were figuring out how to systemize the process.

> *A key to realizing how little work was necessary to do the job well was leaving for an extended period.*

A key to realizing how little work was necessary to do the job well was our leaving for an extended period. It forced Fiona and me to thoughtfully consider which aspects of the job were actually necessary. We did the hard work of renting the place for the year; the rest was just keeping the wheels spinning.

More Than I Bargained For

The following year, my father entertained the idea of buying rental property. He looked at several properties and decided on a 24-unit complex near a technical school. He said he would only buy it if Fiona would manage it for him. He did and she did.

To make it work, Fiona handled the leasing by responding to calls and showing units across town during her lunch break, after work and on weekends.

That first year, I handled the maintenance for my dad's property. As at the Cochrane House, I just delegated any tasks that fell beyond my capabilities. What I didn't realize was how destructive many first-year tech school students can be. They also didn't think it was that important to report maintenance concerns.

I went into an apartment to fix the toilet (which the tenants never cleaned) and saw that the kitchen floor was all spongy. It was obvious to me that the dishwasher had been leaking for quite a while. When I asked the tenants about it, they said, "Yeah it's been leaking for a couple months now. We just put towels around it when we use it."

All I could think was, "Are you serious? Are you really that dense?" That little but persistent leak meant that not only did the dishwasher need to be fixed or replaced, but now the linoleum and subfloor needed to be taken up and replaced, as well. To replace the subfloor, the refrigerator, oven and lower cabinets needed to be removed, and the plumbing to the sink and dishwasher had to be unhooked too—a full two-day, two-person job!

Student housing can be good cash flow, but I didn't realize how much work they can be to maintain until I was responsible for doing the work.

Living Small, Earning Large

Between the two of us, Fiona and I were now making more than $80,000 a year through our full-time jobs and through managing, cleaning and maintaining three apartment buildings on the side. Now, **$80,000 may not sound like a lot to some people,** *but it is a significant amount to someone who has extremely low living expenses!* *We were paying no rent, no phone, electric, gas, or water utility bills, no car payment* and *nothing for health insurance![2]* As a result, we were able to pay off all of our debts entirely and start building our nest egg.

Our Monthly Expense Chart[3]

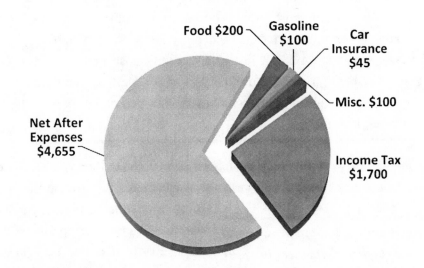

Food $200   Gasoline $100   Car Insurance $45

Misc. $100

Net After Expenses $4,655

Income Tax $1,700

Upon making our last credit payment to the credit consolidation service, they sent us a check for $500, along with a certificate for completing the program. It took another five years to restore our credit to "perfect." It has

---

2 We paid about $3 a month for our amazing health insurance through my university job.

3 Chart is an approximation. We claimed tax deductions from Fiona's business, and I also had a portion of my monthly paycheck put into the University Employee Trust Fund. Either way, our expenses were similar to or less than stated above.

now been perfect for several years. Fortunately for us and for you, old past-due debts and charge-offs do not even show up on credit bureau reports after seven years.

Discovering the Flywheel

We had been at the Cochrane House for nearly two years and had figured out how to get our duties down to about one hour per week during the off-season. There was the occasional clogged drain or running toilet, but things ran quite well with very little effort.

The Flywheel Effect

I call this paring-down and automating tasks, "The Flywheel Effect." You nail down essential tasks; automate what you can, then outsource and systematize the rest. This gets you to a point where you cut down the workload to the least amount necessary to still do a fantastic job. Building the momentum takes the most work. After you have the flywheel spinning, you can just give it a little push now and then to keep it moving in a forward motion. When you start out, you put a lot of time and effort into it, but after a few months you can cut your actual work time drastically.

Fiona and I were now only paying for essentials like food, car insurance and gasoline, and a little for miscellaneous expenses. After getting the okay from my supervisor at work, I started using my work phone as my emergency contact number and cut the expense of my pager service.

Think about not having to pay some of your highest expenses in your life; mortgage, property taxes and utilities. What will you do when you reclaim more of your money?

In a short time, we built a savings account balance of more than $30,000. We knew if we stayed on another year and a half, we would have $100,000 cash sitting in the bank. **We were putting over $4,000 a month into our savings account.**

Late in that second year of managing the Cochrane House, Vince and Mary approached us and asked if we would be interested in buying the property from them on land contract. They had owned the property for over 30 years and were looking to move on to other things.

It was a good price and a great offer at only 10 percent down and the balance on land contract (with no bank involved). We politely declined. In our naïveté we failed to realize that the land would soon be worth far more than the owners were asking for the property.

A Change of Plan

It was only a couple months later that we were notified that the property had been sold to a real estate developer in the area. We were approached by one of the new managers, who told us that our position at the house would no longer be necessary. They gave us a choice between vacating in 60 days or paying $900 a month for rent. We decided to leave, taking it—wrongfully— as our cue to start shopping for our own house.

Upon our departure, Vince and Mary wrote us a wonderful recommendation. A good recommendation is worth more than its weight in platinum. Collect these!

A good recommendation is worth more than its weight in platinum. Collect these!

Looking back, once we had learned Vince and Mary were looking to sell the house, we should have changed our month-to-month contract to a yearly one. It would have given us far more leverage to stay on as resident managers, or to make a new owner negotiate a contract buyout with us.

It didn't take long for us to decide on a house to buy. Once we signed the mortgage papers, it was only a few months before our entire savings was invested into our house. Where did it all go? I was a musician, so I decided to build a recording studio in the basement with what was left over after the down payment.

A Chance at a Dream

We had lived in our new house for almost three years when I approached Fiona with an idea. I wanted to fulfill my dream of completing my music album. I felt that I needed to leave my job at the university to devote myself completely to it. I proposed that we move out and try our hand at resident managing once again.

I knew leaving my job would mean leaving security behind. There would be no way for us to cover house payments, property taxes and utilities on one income. Since Fiona was self-employed, it meant we would also be losing our amazing health and dental insurance. She didn't like the idea of leaving our home. It was our first home, and we had developed a strong attachment to it.

Around that time I went to Mexico on a volunteer house-building trip. I was standing by the half-erected house outside of Juárez when I had a strange urge to check my cell phone reception. Because we were up on a hill, I had caught a strong cell signal from El Paso. I called Fiona to tell her how things were going. She went on to tell me that she had found a great resident manager position in the newspaper, and that we had an interview set up for the day after I returned.

At the interview, the owner sat behind a grand desk while another manager and the property's head of maintenance sat behind us. He asked us questions, and we seemed to be giving the answers they were looking for. In the end, we felt that overall, the interview had gone well.

The property's problem was that out of 34 units, seven were currently vacant. The existing manager was no longer able to fulfill his duties, and the owner needed to replace him as soon as possible.

The owner said we would be responsible for answering calls, renting the apartments, managing apartment turnover, maintaining the cleanliness of the grounds and taking maintenance calls (and then forwarding them to the maintenance team). In return, we would only have to pay $500 a month for a 2- or 3-bedroom town house.

Fiona responded, "How about we pay $100 a month per vacant apartment up to, but not to exceed, $500 a month? That would give us an incentive to keep the place full for you." The owner smiled and said, "I think we can do that."

Shortly before moving into Whispering Hills, we rented out our own house. I knew that there was a recording arts school only three miles from us. So I went to the school and talked to the head of the admissions office. I told him I had heard it was a great school for recording arts and that I had a home with a professional recording studio for rent. I showed him photos and told him about the construction of the studio space. I politely asked if he would be willing to post my flyer in the lounge or let the instructors know about it.

I received a frantic phone message that same day. A student and three of his bandmates were interested in the house and wanted to know if it was still available. I called him back and told him it was. The students took a quick look at the first floor and the studio, and rented it for our asking price right then and there.

A 3-bedroom home in that neighborhood would normally go for about $1,100 to $1,200 a month. Since we had the recording studio space, we were receiving $1,760 a month. The residents were also responsible for paying gas, electric, water and sewer bills and had to keep up the grounds.

That was it! From our first interview for the resident manager position to renting out our house and moving into our free apartment, the whole process took less than 60 days. Even with our poor credit, we now had our own rental property and were landlords.

We were *resident managers* of a 34-unit town house complex, *property managers* of my dad's 24-unit complex and *landlords* of our own rental property, which was netting us about $500 a month. At first, we worked about 8 to 10 hours a week learning the ropes of our new resident manager position, but later things smoothed out.

Fiona took some time organizing the documents and leases. We didn't know anything about the new property. Were there any problem residents?

How did we deal with maintenance requests that were over a month old? We wanted to come in with a strong presence, so that the residents knew we cared, and it took some time to get everything up to speed.

In about three months we were down to only one vacancy. However, many of the leases were ending in the winter, which made it quite hard to rent them that year. Eventually, we learned to have all leases end in the high season in the fall, when students were starting school.

Eight months later, we took the equity out of the house we were renting out to the band and bought another house. Soon, we built another recording studio in it and rented it out to more musicians from the same school.

Once you find the formula, you just repeat it.

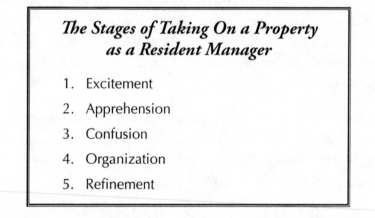

The Stages of Taking On a Property as a Resident Manager

1. Excitement
2. Apprehension
3. Confusion
4. Organization
5. Refinement

A New Life

Travel was important to us. When we designed our system, we wanted to be able to step away from it when we wanted to. It was perfect for the flexibility and mobility-conscious lifestyle we desired.

I've also been fortunate enough to serve others by taking part of missions projects in Juárez, Mexico—building homes for families who were living out of a car or in shacks made of cardboard, chicken wire and pallets. In one week our team was able to build two solid, respectable homes—shelters from the heat and cold, giving those families security, with doors that lock and electricity. I was fortunate enough to be able to pay my own way, without raising funds for the second and third trips.

Chances are you're either on a get rich slow scheme or a keep broke painfully-slow and for the rest of your life scheme.

We've saved literally tens of thousands of dollars in rent and have invested it in many ways. As of November 1, we had saved more than $125,000 in housing and utility costs.

Six years have passed at our current property. We now have two beautiful children, who were born while we were managing. We kept everything going the whole time, through our travels and childbirth.

The model I discuss in the following chapters has given us the freedom to travel, follow our dreams, invest in real estate and spend more quality time as a family.

If you want *true freedom*, you DO NOT want to...

- be stuck with a house mortgage
- be stuck with rising property taxes
- be stuck paying for major house repairs
- become addicted to costly home improvement projects
- be stuck in long-term apartment rental contracts
- flush thousands of dollars down the drain month after month, year after year

Living on-site as a resident manager has many of the privileges you are looking for. Is this a get-rich-quick scheme? Well, define "rich," and then define "quick."

You must go into being a resident manager with the understanding that 70 to 85 percent of the work is up front. Figuring out everything and systematizing your responsibilities may be the hardest part of the job.

If you set up this system correctly, it can mean total freedom for you and your loved ones. The beauty of this system is that it works anywhere in the world.

We want the remainder of this book to be your step-by-step quick-start guide to managing a single rental property of between 8 and 50 units. We will briefly discuss how you can streamline, automate and outsource the processes as much as is humanly and technologically possible.

If you set up this system correctly, it can mean total freedom for you and your loved ones. The beauty of this system is that it works anywhere in the world.

If you are ready to set up a nearly automated system that allows you to **become debt-free, build a sizable nest egg** and **live life on your terms**, you owe it to yourself to read on.

Change Your Thinking

You must get out of your mind the notion that being a resident manager means you can't afford a house of your own or that you are poor or a moocher. Holding resident manager positions has allowed us to own multiple houses and acres of real estate in a foreign country. We pay for vacations with cash, have a diverse investment portfolio and, most important, have the free time to do what we want.

Chapter 2

OWN, RENT OR FREE: UNDERSTANDING THE REAL COSTS OF HOUSING

I'm about to forever change the way you think about the overused, over-inflated phrase "the American Dream" as it relates to home ownership. The esteemed American physician, professor, lecturer, and author Oliver Wendell Holmes once said, "The mind, once expanded to the dimensions of larger ideas, never returns to its original size."

Home Ownership

Owning a home after years of renting and saving is just one of three options. And owning a house for the ultimate payoff of selling it decades down the road is an outdated concept. Most people today live in their home for three to five years before *buying up* or just *moving on*. The *buy-then-move strategy* is shortsighted and costly, since you never realize much equity in your home. Even when buying a home for 60 to 75 cents on the dollar, you must keep in mind all of the not-so-obvious costs that wiggle their way into the equation.

It turns out that buying a home at any *price* is not only a monetarily costly decision in the short and long run, but one that can also consume

Owning a house for the ultimate payoff of selling it decades down the road is an outdated concept.

other valuable resources few people consider when shopping for a house.

Here are three key costs associated with home ownership:

1. **Monetary costs**—the money that leaves your bank account and goes toward your house costs
2. **Sweat equity costs**—the physical work and time you spend to maintain and improve the property
3. **Emotional costs**—the mental real estate involved with thinking about the *knowns* and *unknowns* of home ownership

Monetary Costs

If you are like us, when you looked at buying a home through a real estate agent, you told them your budget was, say, $250,000. More often than not, they then showed you homes for $260,000 or $280,000 because they believed those houses had everything you were looking for and that you would probably be able to swing it by finding the right financing. They may have also factored in that many accepted offers are for less than 100 percent of the seller's asking price.

Determining how much house you can afford by using the maximum amount that a lending institution will give you is actually looking at home buying backwards.

Several of us start with a budget set by what the bank says we can borrow. The bank looks at your debt-to-income ratio, your credit score and your credit rating and offers you an amount it feels comfortable risking on you. If you can't put down enough money to secure your loan, they will require that you get private mortgage insurance.

Determining how much house you can afford by using the maximum amount that a lending institution will give you is actually looking at home-buying *backwards*. You need to budget your housing costs as a whole and be comfortable with all of the costs associated with home ownership—your mortgage is merely one portion of that.

Many home owners fail to consider all the costs associated with home ownership. The majority of home buyers—including Fiona and me—look at the sticker price of the home as the cost.

Most people who shop for a house become emotionally attached to it before it is theirs. When the deal is on the table and the mortgage commitment papers come around, they will blindly sign whatever is in front of them.

We voluntarily blind ourselves to the true costs. We may see the low *price*, but forget about the *real costs*. Below is a list of typical home ownership costs:

- Mortgage
- Private mortgage insurance (PMI)
- Property insurance
- Remodeling (the home is never move-in ready)
- Gas utility
- Electric utility
- Water and sewer utility
- Property taxes
- Pest control
- Repairs
- Upgrades to mechanicals (hot water heater, furnace and air-conditioning)
- Landscaping and lawn care
- Appliance replacement
- Assessed value increase = property tax increase

Compared with the possibility of investing the money into other opportunities, the costs of owning a house far outweigh the potential returns from a sale in the distant future. If your housing were free, what you would have spent every month on it becomes opportunity money—free for you to do with what you like.

It is true that the investment of cash doesn't have the same leverage that a real estate mortgage has. Yet cash gives you the ability to move money around to different funds, stocks or even investments in other markets almost instantly.

Sweat Equity Costs

When you choose to buy a house, your *sweat equity cost* can go up dramatically in the short and long run. That time would have been allocated to other activities if you had kept renting—activities like family time, travel, and hobbies. Some of that time is now invested in your house. If you are a parent, you know exactly what I mean. Fiona and I have often wondered, *What the heck did we do with our time before kids?*

Being a first-time home owner is a lot like having your first child. Everyone tells you how life will change when you bring that newborn home. However, it isn't until you come home for the first time that you begin to realize the scope of the commitment you have made.

> *The truth is that I signed up as maintenance man and groundskeeper when we signed the mortgage papers for our house. I never considered the time it would take to fulfill these responsibilities.*

When Fiona and I took on our current resident manager position, my monetary cost and sweat equity costs went down dramatically. Here is a list of some things I did consistently as a home owner:

- Mow my lawn with a push mower every seven days
- Water the plants and flowers twice a week
- Landscape the yard
- Trim trees every year
- Prune hedges seasonally
- Place 50 bags worth of cedar chips around the house every year
- Rake and bag leaves several times each fall
- Clean twigs and leaves off the roof four to five times each year
- Clean out the gutters twice a year

- Shovel the snow from the walk and driveway and salt it down several times per week every winter

The truth is that I signed up as maintenance man and groundskeeper when we signed the mortgage papers for our house. I never considered the time it would take to fulfill these responsibilities.

When we first considered buying a house, I figured we would need a lawnmower and a tool or two. Not being much of a gardener or handyman, it never occurred to me that I'd start to have thoughts like:

- This place needs flowers in some pretty pottery.
- Is that tree *all* dead or just *mostly* dead?
- Maybe those shutters should come down.
- The paint looks terrible under those shutters; we need to paint that area to make it look right.
- I don't like the color of this house after all. It needs to be painted anyway.
- Why is our lawn covered with little purple flowers?
- Why is there water in the basement?
- Is that a tree growing in my gutter?
- You mean I have to get up on a ladder and *dig* those decaying leaves out of the gutter?
- I have no clue if those are weeds or flowers in the planters.
- You mean we have 24 hours after a snowfall to shovel and salt the public sidewalk before we get a citation from the city?
- Can sealing the driveway wait a few more years?
- Why is the garage door not going up or down, and why is it tilted like that?
- So what you're saying is that if we don't replace our furnace filter regularly, we'll burn out another motor?
- No one told me I needed a building permit!

Emotional Costs

After all of that, there is another cost Fiona and I have encountered—and still do to this day. The *emotional cost* of worrying about the *knowns* and the *unknowns* of home ownership.

Knowns are things you can easily gauge in advance (but try not to think about):

- Mortgage payments: $14,000 a year
- Property taxes: $3,600 a year
- Insurance: $600 a year
- Equipment and supplies to maintain and care for your home: $1,000 a year

The *emotional cost* of *unknowns* can weigh even heavier on you. These are the things that surprise you out of the blue:

- Major home structural projects
- Getting a new furnace, water heater or refrigerator
- Special assessments such as a new sidewalk street or utility project
- Jumps in your home assessment and a consequent property tax spike
- Trying to sell your house in a down market
- Looking for friends and family to help you with projects
- Hoping that your job is secure so you can keep paying for your house

Life has twists and turns. We no longer build homes, raise families and retire in one home.

No matter how much money you put into your house, in the case of a rapid decline in home values—or possibly even worse, your house out-appraising every other house on the block—**the cold, hard fact is that you are never promised you will get your money back out of your purchase**. It use to be practically guaranteed that a home would appreciate, but the housing crash of 2009 disproved that conventional wisdom. And unfortunately, a home

> *Life has twists and turns. We no longer build homes, raise families and retire in one home.*

cannot just be picked up and moved to a better neighborhood to improve its value.

Positive Reasons for Home Ownership

Still, despite all of this negative talk, there are some positive reasons for owning your own home:

- You get a place to call your own. The pride of ownership. No writing rent checks to the landlord anymore; now you write them to a bank. Fortunately, now a few dollars of your payment go toward paying off your house someday.
- Living in a home that is completely paid off is nice.
- You can customize the interior and usually the exterior of your home exactly to your personal taste and standards. No need to ask a landlord if it is okay.
- There may be tax write-offs.
- You can turn up the stereo without neighbors pounding on the wall.
- You may borrow against equity of your home for whatever you want.

But from my experience owning several properties, I have realized there is only one of these benefits I could only derive from owning an *owner-occupied home.*

Should I Own Real Estate?

The truth is, if you invest most of your money in an owner-occupied home, you'll have to wait years and years to realize any gains. Your money is essentially locked up in the house. Unless you use your house like a bank, and borrow against it to buy assets, you'll have to wait until you sell your house to see any money again.

Remember that once you cash out, you'll probably need to find another place to live anyway, and you will be buying at new, inflation-adjusted housing prices. With investments in the right funds, stocks or

continued...

…continued

other paper assets, your money is mobile and accessible with a few clicks, in as little as four seconds and not 4 to 10 months.

There is a lot to be said for owning rental property—which is an entirely different animal from an owner-occupied home. Renters of your properties pay off your mortgage, pay your property taxes and pay for repairs and updates while you reap the rewards. You are providing someone a home with few strings attached, and in return, they build your retirement at a steady pace. Though I don't advocate buying a home to live in with your job income, I think it may be a good idea to buy an owner-occupied home with passive income generated by your assets.

One last thing; I highly recommend holding rental properties in your investment portfolio. Once you have experience resident managing, you will be able to use it to manage your own properties efficiently—or even better, to hire other managers to do what you no longer want to.

Renting an apartment or buying a home can be the right choice for some people at some point in their lives. I recommend that you take a couple hours out of one day and take a bird's-eye view of the next 10, 20 or 30 years of your life in terms of your financial commitment to your housing, because there are better options for most people. **I am not comparing owning a home and renting a home here. I am merely contrasting those two options with the real possibility of <u>not paying anything for your housing—ever again</u>**.

There seems to be a stigma attached to being a renter. It is as if everyone you meet sizes you up by your living situation. Some say with an encouraging grin, Well, if you try a little harder and save, save, save, you'll be able to afford a house of your own someday! It isn't the fact that you're renting as much as the fact that you're not a property owner that makes some home owners feel superior. I know, because I've been on both sides now.

continued…

…continued

I'm here to tell you that home ownership is not all that. It is not the be-all and end-all of living arrangements. Just keep in mind the costs and responsibilities that accompany the pride of ownership of an owner-occupied house.

I'd much rather have the pride of ownership of a great big bank account and investment portfolio than the pride of ownership of a great big house with the great big mortgage and property tax bill that go along with it.

That one benefit was pride of ownership. The decision to purchase a home is usually an emotional one. Starting from when we are young, we are led to believe we need to own a home, and that when we do, we have achieved a modicum of success.

Many house seekers think:

- I can outfit my garage the way I like and finally restore my 1967 Stingray Corvette.
- I'll finally get to have a dog!
- I won't have issues with loud neighbors in a house of my own.
- No more sharing walls with neighbors.
- We can build some financial security for ourselves instead of making the landlord rich.
- No one can tell me what to do!

A Case Study

Let's look at a real life example. Our good friends the Millers have rented different houses for years because of poor credit. They have three children and one or two businesses going at any given time. They found a rural setting for Mr. Miller to do his work.

Both Mr. and Mrs. Miller worked at home. There were even stints of homeschooling. Things were good; however, their house wasn't exactly the way they liked. It was an older home, and the windows were drafty. They would have redone the small kitchen, updated the bathroom and remodeled the basement if they could. They always were telling us how they wanted a home of their own. My question to them was: *Why?* I owned one at the time, and I was realizing it wasn't all that. Sometimes it was a pain in the neck!

They actually had it pretty good. Like most of us, though, they were looking for the greener grass on the other side of the fence. If they could only get that loan, they could get a home of their own. The fact of the matter was that they were renting a house that had many of the benefits that people look for when purchasing a house, *yet they didn't hold the liabilities that go with home ownership.*

For instance…

- They were allowed to put nails in the walls (*hundreds* of them).
- They painted their walls.
- They had a large two-car garage that they used as a shop and for storage.
- They had two dogs.
- They had band practice at the house and recorded an album there.
- They ran two businesses out of their home.
- They held business meetings in their home.
- They had no noisy neighbors. (Sometimes *they* were the noisy neighbor.)
- They had an acre lot on a hilltop that backed up to a green area and a stream.
- They paid $800 a month.
- They had virtually no maintenance costs.
- They didn't have to save up for yearly property taxes every month.
- They didn't have any surprise maintenance costs.

I'd much rather know that every month, like clockwork, I just need to pay $800 for rent—end of story, no surprises. When times are financially tight and you are having problems coming up with mortgage and property taxes, and then the furnace goes out on you, in many cases you are left pleading your case with a bank.

That said, renting may be less expensive when figuring in all the costs of home ownership—but as renters, aren't we just throwing money away? If you have rented, you know the feeling of throwing hard-earned money out the window month after month, year after year, for your housing. That is what led you to look into owning a home in the first place.

Renting – Pros and Cons

On the first of each month, you start over again at zero. Renters can't build equity as home-owners can. The benefit of renting is that you get a nice place to call home without all the work and responsibility of maintaining it. If you are lucky, you have good neighbors and a quiet life.

Paying rent is like staying at a Holiday Inn without the room service. Some *hotels* are nicer than others. Some people pay $270 a night ($8,000+ a month) for an exquisitely furnished *hotel* on Manhattan's Upper West Side. Others pay $20 a night ($600 a month) for rural, drafty *accommodations* in Medford, Wisconsin. My point is that either way, renting is temporary; it will never be *yours* someday. Don't feel discouraged.

If you are renting now, you're not alone. Early 2008 statistics show that about 32 percent of Americans rent.[4] I foresee the percentage of non-homeowners will continue to increase dramatically due to the uncertainty of post 2009 the housing market. The glitter of the *owner-occupied home as an investment* is gone for the time being.

That said; if we were to merely take an average cost per month of a rented apartment, town house or home of $1,250 a month, you can see that $15,000 per year is a remarkable amount of *after-tax* income that can never be reclaimed.

---

4 http://www.huduser.org/periodicals/ushmc/fall08/USHMC_Q308.pdf

Many experts suggest that we should not exceed 30 percent of our *gross* income for housing. Let us say that a third of your income—which is to say roughly a third of your work time—is designated to providing shelter for you and your family:

Gross Yearly Salary: **$50,000**
Gross Monthly Salary: **$4,167**
30% of Gross Monthly Salary[5] (designated for all housing costs): $1,250
Yearly Cost for Housing: $1,250/month x 12 months = $15,000/year

Of course, those monthly rental numbers will be significantly higher in hot metropolitan areas like SoHo and significantly lower in rural La Grange, Kentucky. But in either case, your rent money can never be recovered. You cannot spend or reinvest it; it's gone.

The upside to renting is that you don't have to pay for any little problems that arise. You do not pay to repair or replace items that have outlived their usefulness, like the olive-green oven that no longer heats your casseroles— at least, not directly. Keep in mind that even though you see the owner or manager taking care of such problems, their way of recouping those costs to maintain their investment is to increase rent prices a little more every year.

Don't own, don't rent, don't despair. There is a better way. And as with repairs, another upside is that rising property taxes don't immediately affect you as directly as they do the property owner. Unlike the owner, you can veto the higher taxes much more easily by picking up and moving somewhere else.

Don't get me wrong here: You and your neighbors are paying all of the property taxes with your rent; when taxes go up significantly, the monthly rent will also rise, to help the owner keep his investment at a comfortable rate of return. But you have signed a contract with an agreed-upon rent price, and upon the termination of that contract, you may choose to leave instead

---

5   We have found that 30 percent of either net or gross salary may be used. What we know is that when the term "housing cost" is used, in most cases it is only referring to the monthly mortgage or rent payment. Some personal financial strategists will tell you to overestimate your costs by at least 15 percent to arrive at a more realistic number—so to figure out the actual cost, we are using gross.

of paying the increase in rent. As a renter, you're not hit with the increase in property taxes in the form of a letter stating that $2,500 or $5,000 is due in 30 days.

Renting also allows you a more flexible lifestyle. Many rental properties provide all of the services that take up so much of a home-owner's time. As a renter, you simply come and go as you please, pay your rent on time, and the building and grounds are taken care of for you. You don't have the burden of mowing the lawn, shoveling the snow and cleaning out the gutters. When you go home, your time is *open to other opportunities.*

Renters are more mobile, too. If you are faced with a job transfer or another major life change and need to break your lease, the most you might be out is the remainder of your rental contract. (However, you are usually given the option to sublease your unit either on your own, or by contracting the management company to show and sublease it for you.) Finally, as a renter, if property values plummet—as they recently did for millions of home-owners in the United States—you are protected.

But even though both renting and owning offer some benefits, I believe that the *third option* is a far better route to pursue as a long-term investment strategy.

Don't own, don't rent, don't despair. There is a better way.

Don't Own, Don't Rent, *Live FREE*
A no-cost home is within reach!

I say neither owning nor renting is the best option. No matter what your lifestyle, no matter what your ambitions or dreams are, the best way to achieve those financial dreams on a lightning-fast track is to ***pay absolutely nothing for your home***. Housing is your biggest cost and the biggest drain on your bank account. It *sets the governor* on your lifestyle.

You read it right. FREE HOUSING! What would it be like to have an extra $600 to $2,500 every month to invest in whatever you choose?

I'm not talking about *boomeranging* and moving back in with Mom and Dad, or *couch-surfing* across the country from friend to friend. Sure, nomadic life can be great for a time. Young adults can couch-surf all they want in their single days. But it is not a sustainable living situation for the rest of your life. At some point, you need to have a *home base*—a place to land that isn't your parents' house.

This isn't about taking on three roommates or sharing a home with an elderly person or any other type of *temporary* living situation, either. I'm not interested in temporary—I have a wife and two toddlers, and I value my privacy too much to have even more roomies. I am talking specifically about finding a long-term, low-stress resident manager position *that you control.*

Like most people, when you hear the term *resident manager*, you probably think of headaches such as late-night phone calls, angry tenants, broken toilets and in general a *nightmarish ball-and-chain situation*. And if you were to work like many resident managers do today, I would wholeheartedly agree with your assumption.

However, my wife, Fiona, and I have had an entirely different experience as managers for the last nine years. You see, if you are *lazy-smart*, every part of the resident manager's job can be systematized, automated or outsourced. It took us a few years to figure this out, but since then we have been able to take full advantage of:

- Holding a full-time job
- Running our own businesses off-site and at home
- Following our dreams of making music, filmmaking, teaching and writing
- Traveling to the far reaches of the earth for extended periods
- Having more quality family time
- Helping people with our time and finances

As far as the amount of time that we put into actively working as resident managers, *last year it was around 50 hours. **That's a total of 50 hours FOR***

THE YEAR to manage a 34-unit complex! That is like working one week full-time to pay for your home for the rest of the year!

When I started tracking the time I spent actively working as a resident manager, I realized I had previously spent about *300 percent more time* caring for the lawn and grounds at my former house! Now, I'm happy to say I haven't had to mow a lawn in a very long time!

The system we have developed has allowed us the freedom to do what we want, when we want, while giving our residential community and the property owners who employ us plenty of reason to love us and to never want us to leave. We are not only talking about free rent, utilities, phone, Internet and parking, but also thank-you cards from residents and the management company, gifts, bonuses, parties and more. This system works, and Fiona and I have taken the last several years to fine-tune it. As a matter of fact, it works so well for us, we knew it was about time we started sharing our system for success with the rest of the world.

Learn to Save Time by Following Someone Else's System

What took us years to realize and then systematize takes the students we teach a fraction of the time. The value of our system is that you can choose to avoid much of the struggle by simply doing what we did right and avoiding what we did wrong.

Chapter 3

SO YOU DON'T BELIEVE THE PREMISE? CYNICS, START HERE!

Depending on where in the world you are reading this book, you may call what we do to keep our free home being a caretaker, house sitter, house manager, estate manager, super, superintendent, resident assistant, building warden, concierge, host, resident hall assistant, property manager, building manager or resident manager. Here in the U.S. at the property where we live, Fiona and I answered an ad for a *resident manager* position. However, we have found that what we do is quite different than what most resident managers do on a daily basis.

Because Fiona and I have managed hundreds of units in several different locations over the past 11 years, we have developed methods that have dramatically streamlined our work schedule. What do I mean?

Many resident managers:

- Have no education in managing people or property
- Have undeveloped people skills
- Don't understand how to market effectively
- Hold office hours daily
- Answer calls at all hours of the day and night

- Are the resident fix-it person
- Are responsible for 24-hour emergency maintenance issues
- Can't leave the property for extended vacations
- Have limited or no computer skills

With all of the stereotypes about what resident managers do, we realized it was time that we separated what *we* do from the old way of resident managing and identify a term that better describes our style. That is why we now use the term **Community Executive**. A Community Executive:

- Has been educated in basic management of property and residents
- Understands and uses cutting-edge marketing methods
- Works toward holding few or no office hours each week
- Returns calls at a time convenient to him or her
- Directs staff or contractors who handle maintenance and cleaning
- Uses an on-call 24-hour maintenance service
- Finds qualified substitutes to fill in when he or she plans to leave the property for vacations
- Uses the latest technology to streamline management and to work remotely when necessary

---

How I Will Use The Terms Resident Manager And Community Executive In This Book

Throughout the book I will refer to our approach and the systems we use to manage multi-unit properties and residents in an on-site situation as being a **Community Executive rather than a resident manager**. I will continue to use the title **resident manager** to indicate the type of position to search for and fill, and also when I refer to how most on-site, multi-unit resident managers operate without our system.

I know many people will read this book and believe our lifestyle and the positions we discuss here are neither realistic nor even obtainable by the common person. That is why I wrote this chapter just for you.

Fiona and I have gone to great lengths to write this book for the person who has no training in managing residential properties. We also provide a detailed plan that will help you land a great resident manager position, just as we have.

Following is a list of the most common excuses we hear as to why people wouldn't seek a resident manager position and my response to each objection:

Excuse #1: I love my house; I don't want to leave it. Are you stressed about making housing payments, utility payments, credit card or school loan payments? What is it worth to you to see your debt disappear much faster? We left our house to become resident managers—but we didn't *sell* our house. I wanted to pursue music and to expand our businesses, but we wanted to keep our house in case we ever wanted to move back. We rented it out to have other people pay all of the monthly costs associated with that house. When you become a Community Executive, your paycheck won't have to be stretched so far.

I know this may sound cruel or out of touch, but ***it's just a house***. Would you rather live in your own house and worry more about debt and monthly payments or worry less and pay no housing costs whatsoever?

Excuse #2: I can't do this; I don't have any experience. First of all, ***Fiona and I did not have any experience when we started***. We had terrible credit and didn't know anybody within a thousand miles of where we lived. The management company that hired us didn't look at our experience—they looked at our character. We didn't receive training from them, nor did we *read any manuals* on how to be a good resident manager. It wasn't until years later that we looked into getting basic training. If you are honest, dependable and trustworthy, you can learn everything you need to. Learn from our experience and **let us train you!** We offer online training courses and live seminars for people who are serious about landing the job, doing the job and keeping it for as long as they wish.[6]

Excuse #3: I don't want to change careers or quit my job just to fix toilets. You do not have to quit your full-time or part-time job if you have one. As a matter of fact, our approach recommends that you keep your job for now. We have worked full-time jobs while holding each of

6 Go to www.CommExAcademy.com.

our three positions as resident managers. Most of our jobs were *Monday-to-Friday, nine-to-five–type* jobs. Until recently, Fiona and I were working eight-hour-a-day jobs and managing our community at the same time. We rarely work on weekends, and residents and prospects have learned to work around our schedule.

Let me also clarify one other thing: I have heard so many people say they would never be a resident manager *because they don't want to fix toilets.* The truth is that for the last six years, **I have not fixed any toilets.** I have a maintenance team for that. If our toilet doesn't work, I call maintenance or a plumber. I find it even funnier hearing that excuse from people who own their own homes—*as if the toilet in their own house never breaks!* They tell me they want out of their mortgage, but these little excuses stop them from taking action. It turns out that **we actually do less work as Community Executives of 34 units than we did maintaining our own house!**

Excuse #4: These incredible opportunities no longer exist. Resident manager positions are listed in newspapers and on websites all around the world. They may not appear every single day in your local market, but keep looking, and you will find them here and there. Besides that, this book concentrates on being proactive in your search—creating a position where there may not be one at the present time. Most of these positions are never even listed. They are found through networking or through your persuasive words. I recently read that 70 percent or more of job openings are never advertised.[7] This means you are limited more by your creativity than you are by what positions are on a listing.

It is very possible for those who follow the steps here to land a position that suits their needs and desires. In this book we will teach you what to seek, what to watch out for and how to negotiate your work-in-trade (work you will do to get reduced or free rent) to gain the most possible from your position.

The duties at our first position were simple: Answer the phone, book appointments, show the model apartment to people who stopped by, and

---

7 http://www.computerworld.com/s/article/9141588/7_Tips_for_Job_Seekers_During_the_Holidays

heat cookies. A monkey would have been able to perform most of the tasks; it just would have cost the management company a lot more.[8]

Excuse #5: There are not enough positions for everyone to do this. There are probably a million people applying for these positions. Unfortunately for property owners, there are actually few people who apply for these positions. Many of those who do lack a strong work ethic, a winning personality or the integrity to do the job *well*. You will see some positions posted over and over and over again. I see it as an indication that the poster has yet to get an applicant whom she feels is qualified to do the job well.

Many owners hang on to their resident managers because they fear the hiring process. They know the quality of most applicants, and it isn't a sunny picture. They settle for the status quo over trying to reduce vacancy rates.

The fact is that only 68.9 percent of U.S. residents own their house.[9] That means that almost **100 million** people in the U.S. *do not own* the dwelling they live in. There is a huge need for quality people to manage the dwellings that those 100 million people rent.

This is also true outside the U.S. If you live overseas or are looking to live outside the U.S., the principles in this book transfer to other countries just as well. There will be a few local tweaks and adjustments to consider, but the basic need is the same.

Excuse #6: I'm busy enough as it is. I don't have any time. If you didn't have to make that $1,000-a-month rent payment, could you get rid of your second job? If you kept your second job, would you be able to get out of debt even faster? What about saving for a big purchase like a wedding or car, or taking that money and investing more of it? Because $12,000 a year can be a lot of money to put toward another opportunity. Multiply your current housing payment by 12 to see what kind of raise you could receive if you didn't have to pay for your housing.

Monthly housing cost of $_____ x 12 months = **instant** $_____ yearly raise

---

8 Rent a monkey from Steve Martin's Working Wildlife: http://www.workingwildlife.com
9 2008 numbers: http://en.wikipedia.org/wiki/Homeownership_in_the_United_States

Excuse #7: You cannot leave your resident manager position for weeks on end if you are hired to watch over a property. You are right—most resident managers cannot. However, Fiona and I *can* when functioning as Community Executives. We travel all over the world for extended periods of time. When we plan to leave, we prepare by working harder before our departure; we set everything up and find suitable replacements to handle an abbreviated list of duties. It is truly amazing how a good system will allow you to accomplish so much in so little time.

Excuse #8: You can't outsource everything—there is still a lot of work to do as a Community Executive. Really? The owner or property management company outsourced all of this work to you. Surely elements of your position can be farmed out to others for the short or long term. Can you get a neighbor to shovel snow and salt the sidewalk for you at $10 to $15 each significant snowfall? Could you train a trusted friend to show vacant units for $15 a showing or $50 for every signed lease? Would you pay your assistants $200 for the freedom to be gone for a couple weeks? You bet!

You are right; there is work involved. Much of the work you do depends on your initial work-in-trade agreement and your relationship with the owner or management company. Most important, though, it all comes down to you. If the agreed-upon list of duties is not completed satisfactorily, you are responsible.

For the great benefits we receive, we currently average four hours per month actually managing the property. How much time should it take to fill out a work order form, fill out lease paperwork, show an apartment and pick up trash on the grounds per month? If you allow 30 minutes for filling out lease papers, 10 minutes for cleaning up the grounds, and 10 to 15 minutes a day to check voicemail, return phone calls and post work orders, you can get a lot done in a short period of time.

Sadly, most resident managers feel as though they are *babysitters* or *mother hens* of the property and oblige themselves to sit on the nest. Frankly, I would never take a position that required that. If you stop what you are doing every time a resident needs something, answer every phone call or email that comes in, or chat with the residents for 90—or even ten—minutes whenever you see them, resident managing can take up a lot more of your precious time.

On the other hand, is it worth an hour or two, or even three, each week out of your life to not pay anything for your home?

We do realize that some resident manager agreements are not as good as ours. Your benefits are set in the negotiations of the work-in-trade agreement when you are initially offered the job. With a little guidance from us, however, you can net an amazing return on the time and effort you invest. If you know how to negotiate correctly, you can get a much better return than is listed in the advertisement.

Excuse #9: I don't want to lose my privacy. You learn to set boundaries. If you lose your privacy, it is not your residents' fault. It is your fault for not setting up hours and methods of contact. We rarely have people stop by our door. They know to call or email us. Don't get people in the habit of knocking on your door just because they see your light is on.

Excuse #10: I don't want another job. I just want to come home and relax. We have set boundaries well. We make our voicemail, website and email work for us 24/7.

Depending on the terms you negotiate for your work-in-trade, you may work as little as 10 to 20 minutes a day like we do. Other jobs may take even less—water the plants three days a week, vacuum the hallways, and wheel the trash out to the curb every Sunday, and collect rent checks and mail them to the owner once a month. Every position is unique.

Intermission

DO YOU EVEN QUALIFY TO DO THIS?

What type of person makes a successful Community Executive? Well, the fact that you are reading this book has *drastically* improved your chances. The skills you have acquired through life are the perfect raw materials that, when coupled with determination and a little hard work, will enable you to quickly grow into a fantastic Community Executive. You don't need to have a background in real estate sales, be a retail manager or be an experienced handyman.

Truthfully answer the questions below and find out how well you rank. Don't force your answers to match any trend you notice, just answer what your gut tells you.

1. I am an independent worker.   Yes | No
2. I believe calculated risk can be both safe and rewarding.   Yes | No
3. I enjoy working with people.   Yes | No
4. I can be a clean and neat person.   Yes | No
5. I can put forth a professional image.   Yes | No
6. I can be prompt.   Yes | No
7. I enjoy a challenge.   Yes | No
8. I don't complain—I change.   Yes | No

9. I am a positive, "possibilities" person.   Yes | No

10. I am organized.   Yes | No

Total *Yes* Answers: _____

Your Score: _____

1 – 3	You are not ready to be a Community Executive at this time. You have to change your thinking for this to work for you.
4 – 6	Challenge your current assumptions about yourself and your capabilities. Study this book well, and then take this quiz again.
7 – 8	This will be right up your alley. Know the tools and methods presented here, and go for it!
9 – 10	You are a natural! You will inspire others with your success. Go for it!

Count the number of "Yes" responses. Below is a range that will give you a little insight into whether becoming a Community Executive will be a good fit for you, and whether you would be a good fit for a property owner.

Who can be a Community Executive?

- Students
- Recent graduates
- Newlyweds
- Singles
- Couples
- Couples with children
- Single parents with children
- Empty nesters
- Retirees
- Almost anyone!

What qualities does it take to become a Community Executive?

- Good people skills
- Patience

- Reliability and follow-through
- Organization
- Punctuality
- High tolerance for stupidity ;-)
- Cleanliness and neatness
- High standards for self
- Care for your community's well-being
- Pride in workmanship

What kinds of things do Community Executives do?

- Maintain the appearance of the property
- Maintain a peaceful community
- Answer and return phone calls
- Book appointments
- Show units to prospects
- Market property online and in print
- Coordinate contractors
- Deliver various notices to residents
- Accept rent payments
- Accept applications
- Write up lease agreements

If you are ready to make *YOUR LAST HOUSING PAYMENT EVER*, continue on to Chapter 4.

Chapter 4

YOUR DREAM IS
THE BIGGER PICTURE

There is a glaring problem most of us face when we finish high school and head into the workforce: We plunge headfirst into reality and quickly realize that we were not schooled well enough in money management to ever prosper financially. This problem is experienced by GEDs and PhDs alike.

It doesn't stop in young adulthood, either. Many of us go through life and end up as retirees never truly understanding how to use money and accumulate financial wealth.

> The thing is; having a bigger paycheck doesn't necessarily mean that money problems go away. It only changes the scale of the problems.

We're left scratching our heads, using our credit cards unwisely, spending everything we make and getting the biggest house the bank will allow us to have. After that, we finance new cars at APRs that we never take the time to calculate. We take our vacations courtesy of those shiny new credit cards. Then we get married and add a couple kids to the mix.

Of course, babies require baby furniture, baby clothes and 1,001 accessories. At that point, we need a bigger house to hold all of the stuff we have collected over the years. We need a two-car garage to shelter both of our nice cars from the elements. If we decide not to move on to a bigger home, we simply pull equity out of the house and finance an addition. Besides, the interest may be tax-deductible.

Any way you look at it, school doesn't teach you what to do with your money; it simply trains you how to do your job well enough to keep you from getting fired. And actually, most high schools and colleges never even tell you how to land the job you are going to school for.

My reason for devoting several months of my life to put these words on paper is to open your mind to possibilities. Maybe you don't want to be "rich" per se—maybe you just want to be comfortable.

Well, it turns out that in order to be *comfortable*, you have to be *rich*. Think about it. How do you define *comfortable*? I figure that financial comfort has something to do with having more than you need to do what you want. When was the last time you received your paycheck or took a look at your bank balance and thought, *Yes! I finally have all of the money I need to do everything I want. It's time to cash out!*

My guess is that you haven't felt that emotion since you were four years old, licking a blueberry snow cone and holding a balloon, with a pocket full of change. Because once you got a little older and realized what was out there, you could not live with less than what you knew you were capable of attaining. *The American Dream* can keep you grasping for something that is always just out of reach.

For some, enjoying a $6 million home on the coast of Northern California adjacent to an award-winning golf course is within their capability. For others, it may be a 2-bedroom flat in Manhattan with an artist studio space where they can paint. Others may desire a mobile lifestyle where income is derived from real estate or automated online businesses; they may hold their office in the palm of their hand and keep office hours between their morning newspaper and a mochachino three days a week. To them, absolute mobility is the pinnacle of success.

You Can Live Your Dream

I want you to dream like you used to dream—to remember what you wanted to be as a child, what you were good at in high school or even what you enjoyed studying in college. Most of you got out of school and took the first job that seemed like a good fit. You took it because you were capable of doing the job. Somewhere along the way, however, you left your dreams by the wayside. *"No more time for foolish dreams anymore. Besides, what was I thinking? I can't make a living painting portraits of cats!"*

Living your dream takes a little planning and a lot of determination to see it through. I'm living my dream. I didn't wait until I was making $100,000 a year selling socks on eBay or until I found myself living off the interest of $10 million that magically appeared in my bank account. I didn't even wait until my kids left for college, as many reawakened dreamers do. I just laid a little groundwork and went for it.

What were the repercussions of taking such a risk? Well, I didn't starve, I didn't lose my home, my family and friends didn't shun me, and I didn't get my car repossessed.

Again, I just made a decision and went for it. I figured that no one else was going to tell me I needed to go for my dreams. I chose to live not for my friends' approval, nor my parents' approval, nor my boss's—I simply took a calculated risk.

When you take that calculated risk, what you find will amaze you. Your friends and family will envy your tenacity and your willingness to lay it all on the line, to give up the comfort of the security of your job for the unpredictability of the pursuit of your happiness. Stepping out will set you apart from everyone else.

You will inspire others to follow your lead. They will find the greatness buried deep within their hearts, covered by the layers and years of mediocrity. They will say, *If Matthew can do it—and he's not all that smart—surely I can too.*

I'm telling you that you need to go for your dream right now. The clock is ticking, and there is no one who will tell you that you need to live life to your potential. Stop living by the standards people assumed were yours. Do you want to wake up someday 76 years old and look through a thick, dusty book titled *I Wish I'd Done That?*

I'm here to give you a swift kick in the pants! Because frankly, no one else will. You have to at least *give it the old college try*. (I've always wanted an excuse to say that.) However, trying is actually never enough. "Trying" to follow your dream will only prolong your frustration. You must *act* and *persevere* to achieve anything worthwhile in life.

The Pharmacist in 9C

A few months ago I sat next to a young woman on a plane from Minneapolis to Madison. I was just returning from a business event that had got me fired up, and I was still riding the emotional high. The people at the event were all risk takers, achievers, mavericks and winners in life.

I decided to strike up a conversation with the woman. It was one of those times I just had to talk to somebody about what I felt so passionate about before I popped from excitement. That weekend had turned me into a kid again. I felt like I did in grade school the day I discovered I could buy stickers at the grocery store for 10 cents and sell them to kids on the school bus for a quarter. The world was again my oyster. This poor woman had no chance. She was stuck next to me for the next hour and a half.

Tracy had been out of pharmacy school for about a year and was a little underwhelmed with her choice of career. She had taken a job at one of those big chain pharmacies in a town just a few miles from where I live.

I have talked to too many people my age and younger who are just like Tracy. They grew up with dreams of being a dancer, a comedian, a songwriter or a radio DJ. Many of them won awards for their natural and developed talents and received accolades during their childhood. Unfortunately, along their journey they were dissuaded by well-meaning adults who told them that if they followed *that path* they would probably end up broke—that it was too risky or that they weren't good enough to do it *professionally*.

Sadly, some people lose their dream all on their own. Other times, it's because no one ever said, *"I know you—and I know you can do it"* or *"You should talk to Bob Smith; he seems pretty successful at it and he probably has some helpful insight for you."*

Adults tell us to be responsible. Become a doctor, attorney, pharmacist or banker (okay, maybe not a banker). Part of it is because they want you to fly on your own without having to mooch off of them while you "find yourself" or struggle to make ends meet chasing your silly dream. They do want you to be successful, but mostly they measure success strictly by monetary standards. Parents want us to be financially independent. They want the best for us, but they only know the tools they use in their own lives, so they advise us to do what worked for them.

I want youth today to know that they can follow their dreams, live life on their terms and do it all without bumming off Mom and Dad.

I also want middle-aged, burned-out corporate types to know that within the next several months, they can pay down their debt, quit their dead-end job and start pursuing that dream they've waited to live for so long.

I want empty nesters and retirees to know they can regain some security by paying nothing for their home—and possibly even rent out the home they own for added income, too. You can provide for your family and become a responsible, happy grown-up without selling out and living the dreams someone else has set for you.

Anyway, back to my conversation with Tracy.

"So, why did you choose to become a pharmacist?" I asked her.

Tracy replied, "Because they start out making $60,000 to $70,000 per year." (*Duh.*)

I couldn't help but think, *Hey, Tracy—is money your only motivation?* Of course, I couldn't say that out loud. Maybe she had thought her career would be more interesting, that she would have some involvement in cutting-edge medicine. Pharmacy jobs are great, and there's nothing wrong with being a pharmacist. The problem I had was that her *reason why* had a dollar sign in front of it. If you are doing any job solely for the money *and have the option to do other things*, you may be selling yourself short.

In reality, most people make career decisions *before college*, earn the degree and move on to the high-paying salary, *or* they *go to college for one thing* and *get a job in another.*

I asked Tracy a second question: "Are you happy being a pharmacist?" Her raised eyebrow and smirky smile said to me: *Who said I'm supposed to be happy? It's a job.*

"Well, not really. It's okay," she admitted.

"May I ask you another question?" I said. "Have you ever thought of doing something else?"

I could see the jolt in her brain as I said it. She had just spent the last several years of her life training for exactly what she was doing right now— and getting paid a comfortable salary for doing it.

"Like what?" she asked.

I said confidently, "Like maybe starting your own business."

Tracy's reply was one of the reasons I knew I needed to write this book.

"I'm not an MBA. I don't know anything about business," she said shyly.

So many students graduating from high school or college don't realize that they can do anything they set their minds to. Every entrepreneur starts with little to no experience running a business. All they need is an idea and the passion to see that idea come to fruition.

"Humor me for a moment," I said to her. "Did you study a language in high school?"

"I took French for three years," she replied.

"Do you think you could get some workbooks and teach a 12-year-old child basic French?" I asked.

Tracy shrugged her affirmation.

I continued, "Do you think you could charge her parents $10 an hour for doing that?"

"I guess so," Tracy said with a puzzled look on her face.

"What about two kids? Do you think you could teach two at once?"

"Probably." The look in her eyes said, *Where are you going with this?*

"What if you were to have a few fun activities for a group of kids to do while learning French a couple times a week. Do you think you would be capable of doing that?"

She was beginning to see where I was going with this. "I don't know, maybe," Tracy said with a laugh.

"What if you were teaching a group of eight children basic French two times a week at $10 per student per session. That would be $160 a week, right? And how many hours are you actually tutoring?" I asked.

Tracy smiled. "I don't know. Two?"

I went on: "So you are now making $160 for two hours of work a week. Sure, you'll have to put the lessons together the first time you go through the process, but basically you are making pretty good money by most standards."

She was smiling now, realizing that I was showing her how she could easily start a business of her own, without an MBA or a teacher's certificate. As we approached the runway, I wanted to stretch Tracy's mind just a little further.

"Do you think maybe you could find a college student studying to teach French to do your job teaching those kids for two hours a week and pay her $20/hour? If you did, you could make $120 a week just for setting this all up," I said, unable to hide my glee.

Oh, oh—short circuit. I had gone too far. All I saw was brain freeze. And when her brain started to function again, a frown formed on Tracy's face. She was realizing that there would be risk and possibly hard work involved—and for far less than what she made as a pharmacist.

She said, "Yeah, but wouldn't that be taking advantage of them?"

"No, Tracy!" I said. "You'd be providing language training where there was *none* before you started. You would also be providing teaching experience for a college student while they're getting paid well.

"The better you did your job serving the students and their parents, the more people you would attract; and the more you attracted, the more people you would need to hire. The more people you hired, the more experience they would get while getting paid $20 an hour in the process.

"These teachers could use that experience (that you provided them) toward their next job, where they could perform even better. The experience you provided them would actually help them land their next job, and the kids would be getting the additional training they needed. Do you see what I mean?"

Tracy nodded.

"That's just one idea. You can make a business out of anything. You don't have to have a certificate to teach, and you don't need to have majored in business or finance to start a small business," I concluded.

As the plane landed, I could see Tracy's mind was reeling. She was probably making $60,000 or more at the time of our conversation. This professional in her mid-twenties was working a clean, no-sweat-required and comfortable 40 hours a week.

She may have thought that I was suggesting that she leave her job and start a language school the next week. And her high-paying job with the big company provided a lot of security for her. She had all of the benefits *and* the retirement package, and here I presented a threat to her financial security. Nothing I could have said that night would change her mind about that. But I merely wanted her to think about *possibilities* and look at things from outside the box.

Starting a business when you have income you're already earning as someone else's employee greatly improves the possibility of your venture being a success. Tracy was in the perfect position to start her business. Once you have an income stream, you just need to define how the money will exit your bank account. You have to invest in the right places.

> *Starting a business when you have income you're already earning as someone else's employee greatly improves the possibility of your venture being a success.*

It is one hundred times more difficult to start a business without a job or cash flow and little to no money to invest to get it started. Even worse is to have no job and to be in debt and to want to start a business. Worst of all is to have to pay for housing, to have little to no income and no savings and creditors calling, while trying to stay excited about your new business venture. I know because that is where Fiona and I started.

I've been at the bottom. I've been at zero cash into my bank account with collection agencies calling me every night asking when they would get their money. I've started businesses with no money, and it isn't easy. I've been there at the gas pump, carefully metering out $5.34 worth of gas into the tank.

You need to look at your job as a gift. Many people love their job and find fulfillment in what they do and the fact that they get paid to do it. If you have a job, consider yourself blessed. I am talking here to those people who know they are not living the life that deep down they believe they could—people who are not finding fulfillment in what they are doing now.

However, keeping a job you may not necessarily enjoy is critical to getting yourself out of debt quickly and building a portfolio of diversified investments. It all starts with a dream and a plan. Becoming a resident manager and paying nothing for your home will allow you to pay down your debt and build financial security much faster than what you are doing now. You are working hours of your life each and every year to pay for your housing; why not work far less and make far more?

Let this be your wake-up call to alert you to some of the possibilities available to you. Forge ahead and pave new roads for yourself. It's time to build a lifestyle that gives you the freedom to do what you want, with a firm financial foundation. Get ready to *live life on your terms*.

LANDING
THE POSITION

Chapter 5

SITUATIONS TO LOOK FOR: SEPARATING THE FANTASTIC FROM THE FRUSTRATING

Opportunity knocks, not once, not twice, but many times throughout the day. The problem is that we focus on the minutiae and not on what really matters. This was never more evident to me than when I heard it from Armand Morin.

Armand is an Internet Marketing legend. Once on a phone call I asked him, "What is the one overarching skill you have developed over the last several years that has allowed you to achieve financial success on the level you have?"

His answer was simply, *"I've learned to observe the world around me."*

I believe Armand not just because I know him as a great, down-to-earth guy on a personal level, but also because he has proven his methods by grossing $25 million in revenue last year with only seven employees.

You must learn to observe the world around you. Opportunities are truly everywhere. Some are right in the room where you are reading this book. Many of us have blinders on because we go through the routines of everyday life and stay comfortable.

It takes effort and creativity to see the opportunities. They hide in almost every conversation you have. In this case, the Community Executive opportunity you are looking for is probably right in your neighborhood. More than likely, there is also a great opportunity in the neighborhood where you would *like* to live—regardless of the city, state or country it's in.

Finding the Right Position

First off, let me save you a lot of misery by listing telltale signs of *what you do not want* to find.

Situations to avoid:

- Properties with high vacancy (30 percent or more).
- Bad neighborhoods—if you wouldn't feel safe walking the neighborhood at, don't manage it!
- Young or new-to-the-industry owners with seemingly little operating budget or reserve cash. They will not understand why some things are worth spending money on, such as improvements to the building or grounds. Or they may understand the importance, but lack the funds to do it right.
- Stingy or ornery owners/managers who ask you for a lot but give you very little in return. They will not be reasonable to work with and will want more out of you all the time.
- Owners with multiple lost lawsuits against them—check the owner's name or the property management company's name against www. bbb.org and your local court records.
- Properties that are falling apart. Disrepair tells you how little the owners really care. If they have no pride in the well-being of their investment, how much will they care for you? *Will they expect you to raise the Titanic?*
- Properties that rely mostly on month-to-month or transient residents (unless the units are furnished executive apartments or suites). You are not looking to manage a hotel.

- Owners who complain about how little they have. If the owner seems to talk about how he can't afford to repair the roof, says things like "I'm not made of money" or in general seems *cheap*, keep away.

- Owners who are overwhelmingly negative. You will never be good enough to please them.

- Owners who belittle the current or previous resident manager, placing *all the blame* for their misfortune or low occupancy on them alone.

- Owners who cannot see any faults with their property. Some are blind to flaws that may be turning people away—and remain blind even when you mention your concerns.

- Properties that advertise more than one month free when tenants sign a one-year lease. I've seen up to three months free. This shouts desperation. You have to wonder why they are so desperate. Not a good first-time assignment.

- Properties that allow large dogs. Dogs can be very destructive. I have yet to see a security deposit that fully covers the property damage a dog can do.

- Owners who like to micromanage. They will call you all the time to see what you're up to.

Situations to Seek:

Of all the resident manager positions available, advertised or not; following these tips will save you hours of time pursuing the wrong opportunities.

- Properties between 8 units on the low end and 50 units on the high end.

- Outgoing owners—people excited about life, who understand fluctuations in the rental market and are excited at the possibility of you being a part of their team.

- Experienced owners—they have had good managers and bad managers and are willing to let you know the difference when you ask them.

- Properties that have been taken care of with pride.

- Properties with low vacancy rates—under 15 percent.
- Properties that are sought-after, or respected or highly rated by previous residents.
- Owners who are realistic about your duties and are generous with what they offer you in return—they will never (or rarely) offer more to you and require less of you than before you accept the offer. Be sure the duties and compensation are crystal-clear before you say yes.
- Long-term residents—residents who have lived on the property for three or more years or lease terms. We've known residents who have inhabited an apartment for more than 30 years.
- Month-to-month lease for you—don't get stuck in a yearlong lease and then realize the position isn't the right fit. The best arrangement requires just a 30-day notice from you to end your lease and, in the other direction, a 60-day notice of termination from the owner.
- Owners willing to put enough money into marketing the property correctly.
- Owners interested in the community's well-being.
- Owners willing to *write down* the terms of your agreement—always a great way to start.
- Owners who want to be hands-off—they trust you to act on their behalf.
- Owners who are organized and experienced.
- Properties with preexisting 24-hour maintenance arrangements.
- Properties with a maintenance team.
- Properties managed by a well-respected management company.

The above are all signs that a property could have the potential to provide you with a long-term Community Executive position.

Where Do You Look for Posted Resident Manager Positions?

- Bulletin board websites (www.craigslist.org)
- Job websites (www.monster.com)
- Local job centers

- Newspapers—some owners are still old-school
- Our website: www.CommExAcademy.com

But what if you can't find any resident manager positions in the area where you want to live? Well, according to author, motivational speaker and master networker David Sherman, *70 percent of all jobs in the U.S. are never publicly advertised.*

According to author, motivational speaker and master networker David Sherman, **70 percent of all jobs in the U.S. are never publicly advertised.**

Where to Proactively Find a Resident Manager Position

We have found that the optimal number of units to manage as a Community Executive is between 8 and 50 units. Anything less can become too costly for an owner. Any more than 50 units tends to become a part-time job situation requiring office hours.

However, we did start as weekend help at a 218-unit property. The management company required very little work in exchange for a 40 percent rent discount of $400, plus pay per hour.

My best advice is to let the owner or management company be the one to say no. Don't prejudge an owner's needs or a deal they may offer before you introduce yourself to them. You don't know the situation until you ask.

An owner may have paid off their 8-unit property back in 1993, and might be eager to move to Florida. The small cost of a competent individual like you managing his investment while he is away may be well worth losing any potential income from the apartment you occupy. The peace of mind is worth the cost to the owner.

Being proactive will really give you the best chance to become a resident manager *on your terms.* One reason is that you are catching the

Being proactive will really give you the best chance to become a resident manager on your terms.

owner or management company off guard. They know you could be a valuable asset, but they haven't taken the time to write up an advertisement outlining duties yet. Just showing interest can give you a tremendous advantage to getting a position over others who never ask.

Where do you find these unadvertised positions?

- Relatives—they may know a property owner or may be willing to introduce you to their apartment manager/owner
- Apartment associations—ask a secretary or assistant if they could let you know which management companies use resident managers or about owners who may be looking for a manager. Some associations have a list of members available to fellow members.
- Properties where you live now or have rented in the past
- Investor's club meetings
- Real estate club meetings
- Campus papers
- Elders at your church, synagogue or other house of worship
- Fraternal clubs like the Elks, Knights of Columbus or Freemasons. Many of the members are older and may have a midsize to large real estate investment portfolios
- Organizations like Rotary or Business Network International
- Chambers of commerce
- If you see a property at a good location, but it looks like management is slacking, contact the owner by looking them up by address on your local property assessor's website. Ask them if they are happy with their current management or resident manager. Tell them you can show them how you would be a good replacement for whomever they're currently using.
- Visit properties that you would like to resident manage and approach the staff of the management company with your résumé (more on that later).
- Place your own ad on craigslist and other bulletin board websites under *Jobs – Real Estate* or *Services – Real Estate*.

Owners of rental properties tend to know each other. When they know someone who is looking for a resident manager, or when they themselves actually need one, they will call you. You will stick in their memory if you have presented yourself as:

1. Responsible
2. Professional
3. Energetic
4. Politely persistent
5. Personable

People are generally lazy. In most cases, if you have presented the five qualities above, an owner will call you first merely because it is the easiest thing for them to do. Even if you are not the most qualified, accredited or attractive person for the job, sometimes showing initiative is all it takes.

One Man Who Would Rather Keep a Thief as Resident Manager

A doctor friend of mine said that the best resident manager he ever had was stealing about $20,000 a year from him. He didn't fire him because he liked the guy and he did his job well. In other words, he'd rather keep a thief as a manager of his assets than look for somebody new.

Job Description

In your search for a resident manager position, you will find that there are no two alike. What is key is to decipher the intent behind the phrases that are used in the ads. Knowing the intent of what is written in the ad will help you know immediately if the position is a good fit for you and your plans as a Community Executive. Just like anything else, the more experience you have searching ads and talking to owner or property managers, the sooner you will feel which ads are right for you to pursue and which to pass on.

Positive things to look for:

- The words "part-time" or "flexible"
- The words "luxury" or "award-winning"
- Wording that implies a "ma-and-pa-owned" property
- The words "family-owned and operated"
- Words like "quiet community"
- Short ads
- Unsophisticated ads
- Work that can be batched (e.g., cleaning common-area windows, vacuuming the hallway and picking up trash in the parking lot can all be done in one hour on a Saturday afternoon)
- Daily or weekly responsibilities—and not too many of them—you can see a friend being able to easily perform while you are away
- Free rent
- Free rent + hourly pay
- Free rent + hourly pay + lease signing bonuses (they are out there!)
- Seasonal work (shoveling snow from the sidewalk, raking leaves)
- Annual tasks (trimming of bushes, planting flowers in early spring)
- Tasks you know you could have your child do (sweeping and cleaning common areas)

Beware of ads that:

- Are a long list of demands
- Are full of detail upon detail upon detail
- Offer all the compensation in the form dollars for hours
- Shout "anal-retentive" (even if you think you may be too—stay away!)
- Look as if someone had the time to take an entire day to write it (they'll be supervising you later)
- Are long yet ambiguous about the scope of duties
- Seem to be hiding something

Watch out for wording like:

- "Tasks include but are not limited to" or "Other tasks as assigned"
- "Requires ability to work any of the seven days of the week, 52 weeks of the year"
- "*Extremely* critical" (not just "important" or "critical," mind you)
- "Ability to work scheduled hours plus any other hours necessary to complete the job"
- "Subject to change"
- "Fast-paced work environment"
- "Must testify at legal proceedings"
- "Must be on-call 24-hours"
- "Maintenance experience a must"
- "Must enjoy fixing toilets at 2 a.m. while knee-deep in water" ;-)
- "Will never see daylight again" (okay, that may be going a bit too far)

Here is the actual ad layout from the newspaper Fiona responded to six years ago that led us to our free home.

On-Site Resident Manager
34 units. ABC Company
555-1234

There was no way we could have known how amazing the position would turn out to be judging from the advertisement. I've found that the less sophisticated the ad, the easier the owner or manager often is to work with. No matter the listing, contact a lot—even if you just want to gain experience.

So how hard is it to find these positions? Take a look at what I found within about 15 minutes of searching.

Samples of Positions Listed on craigslist

Resident manager positions are listed all over the world online. Just look at websites like craigslist.org under terms like "resident manager" or "caretaker" to find a few.

Before you go looking, know what it is that you are seeking. Define your end goal. What is it you want?

I took a quick look at craigslist today, and here are a few actual listings I found. I have placed my comments after each advertisement. These ads and comments may help you find a position you can be really happy with. More examples can be found at www.CommExAcademy.com/adsamples.

Luxury west side apartment community is seeking a couple/pair to take care of a 30 unit building beginning 4/1.

We take pride in our property, both exterior as well as the interior. Voted Property of the Year in 2007 & 2008 and would like to do so again in 2010! Seeking individuals that don't mind a little elbow grease to make their building shine. Responsibilities include but not limited to; vacuum, dust, window cleaning, cleaning underground parking, tending to dog station, and snow removal. If you think you have what it takes and can keep our residents happy, please submit your resume. No phone calls please.

Location: West side

Compensation: rent credit applied to monthly rent, determined upon experience

Short and to the point. Luxury apartments and property of the year. Notice that it is either seasonal work (snow shoveling) or simple cleaning—which might be possible to take care of in one day every week. No leasing apartments necessary. Compensation is determined upon experience (do they mean cleaning experience?). Have them define what the "...but not limited to" sentence means. Get all duties in writing. Probably about one or two hours of work per week in non-snow season.

Position Rating: 4 out of 5 (Great example.)

Title: On-Site Resident Manager
Dept: Property Management
Location: XXXXX (Must live on-site, apartment provided)
Type: Full-time, Exempt
To Apply: Submit a cover letter with your resume and in the subject line reference Job Code #.

Reporting to Property Supervisor, this position will be responsible for the day-to-day management of the property, overseeing the physical maintenance and upkeep of the property, performing various administrative and clerical tasks, maintaining positive resident relations, and adhering to all applicable governmental rules and regulations.

Duties and responsibilities include:

1. RENTAL ACTIVITIES
   a. Follows the application process as established by XXXX in order to meet funding and legal requirements;
   b. Insures that vacant units are cleaned and in move-in condition within 5 days of resident move-out;
   c. Inserts ads in newspapers, as directed by XXXX;
   d. Responds to prospective resident inquiries;
   e. Interviews and shows vacancies to prospective residents;
   f. Maintains current file of application received and regularly updates the waiting lists of prospective residents;
   g. Conducts timely and accurate background checks of applicants and recommends prospective residents for acceptance;
   h. Works with Property Administrator at XXXX to prepare leases; reviews leases and house rules and regulations with new residents;
   i. Promptly and efficiently follows move-in and move-out checklist items, procedures and policies.

continued...

...continued

2. RENTAL COLLECTIONS
   a. Collects rent when due;
   b. Executes receipts for money collected;
   c. Serves late rent notices, 3 day notices and collects late rent and charges;
   e. Works with XXXX staff to keep accurate and complete rent roll including listings by unit of gross rent potential, rent paid, late charges, non-payment, etc.;
   f. Makes bank deposits of rents and other charges/fees received on a timely basis.

3. RESIDENT RECERTIFICATION
   a. Works with XXXX staff on the annual recertification of residents. blah, blah, blah...

This ad continues for two pages!

Wow! This is a lot to think about. Too much work and too much detail. This sounds like a full-time job that requires you to live on-site. It seems as though this position could literally run your life! It could be good for someone who has experience, is extremely organized and wants to have a full-time, high-stress job. This is the first impression they are making to appeal to people who are looking for work. Not a position I would recommend for your first time out.

Position Rating: 2 out of 5 (Not for first-timers.)

To see several more real ads and my commentary on them, go to **www.CommExAcademy.com/adsamples**

Resident Manager

Reply to: job-xxx@craigslist.org

Resident manager position for apartment complex in Xville. MUST have at least conversational language skills in Spanish. Pay based on experience. Somewhat flexible schedule but must be available for showings. Car helpful but not required since you work where you live!

Call Ken at (xxx) xxx-xxx or email.

Main Responsibilities:

- Answering phone and email inquires quickly and efficiently.
- Taking applications for prospective tenants.
- Preparing new tenants to occupy apartments or existing tenants on move out.
- Setting up showing appointments.
- Tracking ad responses.
- Must possess good communication skills (both oral and written)
- Basic computer skills (email, Word) ability to keep professional behavior with tenants and owners.
  - Location: Xville
  - Compensation: Free apartment and rent up fees and hourly.
  - OK to highlight this job opening for persons with disabilities
  - Principals only. Recruiters please don't contact this job poster.
  - Phone calls about this job are ok.

If you are conversant in Spanish, this could be a great position. All the duties may sound intimidating, but after you do them once or twice, follow the advice given in this book and take additional training if necessary, this job could be surprisingly straightforward. At first blush, the position looks automatable, and the manager seems flexible enough to negotiate with a competent person.

Position Rating: 5 out of 5 (Check for possible lack of mobility.)

I want to demystify the last ad above by translating it sentence by sentence. Knowing what each part of it means may help you understand how to tell if an opportunity is worth considering.

Here is my translation:

Resident manager. You will live on-site with other residents.

Reply to: job-xxx@craigslist.org. You can email me at this cloaked email address.

Resident Manager position for apartment complex in Xville. Here is the city where the property is located.

MUST have at least conversational language skills in Spanish. Know how to speak it as well as you did to pass second-year Spanish in high school. They want to know you can speak to residents about notices and maintenance issues and provide basic descriptions of apartments and terms to potential residents. Some of this could be prewritten. If you are really creative, you could use online and offline tools to help you with fast translations. If you see a lot of ads in your desired area that require bilingual speakers, you may want to think about buying Rosetta Stone software off of eBay and studying the language.

Pay based on experience. We can negotiate your pay depending on how competent you seem, from our first contact to the end of our in-person interview. Any time an owner says "pay based on experience," it is just their way of saying that unless you have years of experience, they're going to start you low and increase your pay a little every year. Don't worry about that—once you show them you are serious and that you have even a degree of relevant experience, you can negotiate up toward the higher end of their pay scale.

Somewhat flexible schedule but must be available for showings. I love to see the word "flexible" describe the position. After a little while, you will be able to book showing apartments according to *your* schedule. But you must demonstrate that you are flexible at first.

Car helpful but not required since you work where you live! Owning a car is not necessary. Ending this sentence with an exclamation mark shows me that this guy is not all serious all the time.

Call Ken at (xxx) xxx-xxx or email. I checked out who Ken is by doing a Google search on the phone number. "Ken Smith" came up as a match for the phone number, and he lives in the area where the ad is listed. I found out he is a Realtor and that he sells investment property. I also learned he has a couple of properties for sale that are big enough to require resident managers. I dug deeper and found out that he also works with a large property management company that specializes in janitorial and maintenance of commercial buildings. This may be an ad for one of the properties Ken owns or a property he needs managed for a client.

Main Responsibilities. Here is what is most important—since the last guy may not have done them well enough for Ken to keep him.

Answering phone and email inquires quickly and efficiently. "Quickly" = within 12 to 24 hours. "Efficiently" = follow through with contact so I don't have to get involved.

Taking applications for prospective tenants. "Hi, thank you for the application!" A drop box would work in many cases.

Preparing new tenants to occupy apartments or existing tenants on move out. Have forms filled out and ready for new residents to sign. Show them where the trash goes, where they can park, the phone numbers for maintenance and emergencies, and your phone number, of course. This could be done with a welcome packet or even a sheet that explains everything to them.

Remind existing residents that their apartment will need to be cleared out and cleaned by noon on the date of move-out. This can be done in writing a week before the move-out date. Note to them that fines may accrue if they stay past the lease end date, since the apartment turnover crew will need to perform maintenance, paint, cleaning the apartment and clean carpets.

Setting up showing appointments. When a prospective resident calls, take down their information and call them back. If they meet the criteria to become a resident (e.g., any special income requirement, no pets, etc.), set up a mutually agreed-upon time for the prospect to walk through the apartment.

Tracking ad responses. When prospective residents call, simply ask where they read or heard about your property and note that. If it was from a resident at the property, be sure to thank and/or reward that resident.

Must possess good communication skills (both oral and written). Applicant must be able to speak clearly and be able to read and write.

Basic computer skills (email, Word). Can you email? Do you know how to use a word processing program like Microsoft Word or a similar program? Great; you qualify.

Ability to keep professional behavior with tenants and owners. Don't fraternize with the residents. Yes, you may talk to them about their apartment conditions and make sure the property meets their standards, and the occasional neighborly chat is okay. But don't date, drink alcohol with, swap conspiracy theories with, argue politics with, overstay your welcome with, yell at or simply annoy the residents. You are there as the face of the company and the owner—keep it friendly, but always professional. I can only imagine why they had to include this.

Location: Xville. The property is in Xville.

Compensation: Free apartment... Very nice. You get a free apartment. Once they say that, you negotiate up from there. They can afford you living there for free.

...and rent-up fees... When you sign a new renter, you receive a bonus. $50 to $150 per renter is not uncommon. It is usually calculated as a percentage of the first-month income for the unit.

...and hourly. You are paid hourly for any tasks that fall outside of the everyday duties we agree to in exchange for free rent. This hourly wage is negotiable.

OK to highlight this job opening for persons with disabilities. We welcome applicants with disabilities who can perform the duties listed.

Principals only. Recruiters please don't contact this job poster. This is only open to those interested in filling the position themselves.

Phone calls about this job are ok. I listed my phone number for a reason. Call me about this position. I would love to talk with you about it. I would rather prequalify you over the phone than take an hour to meet you at the property, only to find out that you don't want to do what I require or are incapable of doing it. By the way, do a reverse phone search and find out more about me!

Do you think you could fill this job listing (language skills aside)?
YES   NO

That is all there is to separating the fantastic from the frustrating.

In closing, be wise about your selection. Look around you for opportunities. Don't only check out areas of town you would like

> *Don't let your* city limits *be your* limit.

to live in; check out cities and countries you have dreamed of someday living in. Don't let your *city limits* be *your limit.*

Don't go to areas that seem dangerous or on the decline. There are too many decent properties out there for you to settle for less. Don't get so desperate for experience that you get yourself into trouble.

As you drive around desirable neighborhoods, write down names and phone numbers of top-end apartment complexes. Find out who manages them. These are the management companies you want to align yourself with, or whose success you want to emulate.

To see several more real ads and my commentary on each, go to
http://www.CommExAcademy.com/adsamples

Chapter 6

BREAKING IN: SECRET TACTICS TO GETTING INTERVIEWED

I will cover two techniques in this chapter. Both are very powerful and will give you a leg up on all of your competition. First, I will tell you **how to approach advertised positions**. These are the opportunities that I discussed finding earlier. Second, I will show you **how to get in on unadvertised positions or create a position for yourself as a Community Executive.**

There are dozens of places to find listings of resident management positions. See the current list at www.CommExAcademy.com/membership. In Chapter 5, "Situations to Look For," I cited several examples and rated the quality of each position, based on the appearance of the ad.

Before you expend your energy investigating every opportunity, be sure you start with the best offerings first. Have your résumé and cover letter ready. Be sure your most relevant experience is listed first. Your cover letter will need to be tailored to every opportunity for which you apply. Also, you will need to determine ahead of time what you will and will not do—make a list. If you don't make a list, you may compromise your standards without thinking it through. Keep your eyes open for a real gem of an opportunity.

A company advertising a job at a beautiful property in a great location, requiring the resident manager to perform a few simple duties in return for a measly $200 off rent, may be negotiated later to net you free rent when you add more value for the owner or management company. If you see that they have sidewalks to shovel, weeds to pull or annual flowers to plant, and you know you can do those things, why not say so while you're negotiating? (More about this later in Chapter 8, "The Art of the Deal.")

Each property and each owner/manager sets up resident manager agreements differently. I have never seen two alike. Since each property requires different duties and contractors to maintain them, you may be able to rewrite the agreement to your liking through proper negotiation.

What You Offer

Everyone has something to offer a property owner. You don't have to be a real estate pro to apply or do the job well. Your experiences have prepared you to figure things out. If you have owned a home, you understand how to care for a property. Following are some examples of what I mean.

Occupation or experience	What the owner may see in your résumé
Freelance photographer	"An independent worker. A creative type that may be able to take some better photos of my property. I bet they would be good at creating better ads, a new brochure and signage for my properties."
Accountant/bookkeeper	"Finally, an analytical professional I can communicate with. They understand how to improve the bottom line. They're trusted by others with money and bank accounts."

Retail/sales associate	"Someone who understands sales and customer service. I can fill those vacant apartments!"
Janitor/custodian	"This person is willing to get her hands dirty. It's about time I found someone who will give this place the attention to detail it needs. First thing we'll do is improve the curb appeal."
Fast-food supervisor	"She leads a team of others. Works quickly and understands implementing a system."
Unemployed home-owner	"She understands yard work, grounds keeping and the importance of keeping on top of maintenance, cleaning and paying bills on a monthly basis. Possibly she has some handy repair skills."
College graduate	"This person follows through and has a well-rounded education she can draw upon when running my property."
Handyman	"Jackpot!" ☺

Write in your occupation or past experience below. What could an owner see in your résumé?

_____

_____

_____

_____

Your Résumé Package From a Marketing Perspective

- **Cover letter = Your sales letter.** Takes recipient from cold to interested. Make it a real page-turner!

- **Résumé = Your benefits and features.** This is a list of what you do well and why you are the best. Gets recipient to take the next step and want to meet you in person.

- **References = Your social proof.** Here are 10 other people who think you're great. Have the recipient read what these others have to say about you.

Writing Your Cover Letter

Don't talk about your wonderful experience working at Acme Corp. for the last 17 years; that is what your résumé is for. Don't talk about your recent layoff, either! This letter is to be clear and pithy; this isn't the place to be loquacious. Just write a short, easy-to-read explanation of why your potential employer should turn the page and look at your résumé. Keep it between half to three-quarters of a page.

First, explain the reason they've received this bit of mail. Write about what you are looking for and how their property or company seems to be a good match for your skills.

> *This letter is to be clear and pithy; this isn't the place to be loquacious. Just write a short, easy-to-read explanation of why your potential employer should turn the page and look at your résumé. Keep it between half to three-quarters of a page.*

Give them a good reason to contact you. If you're contacting them by email, the body of the email can be your cover letter. Don't be shy about requesting an interview—it is the whole reason for sending your résumé package in the first place. Mention that you will be following through shortly. And when you say you will follow through, do so. There is nothing worse than finding a talented person who doesn't follow through.

Your cover letter is essentially a sales letter—with *you* as the product. Don't sell yourself on the first page; just warm them up. Make yourself relevant to their needs and tell them why you are the right person for the job by using the words they use in their advertisement. Be smart about it, and don't parrot their job description word for word.

If they posted a position in an ad, be sure to reference it. Use their terminology and be specific. Don't ramble on. If they are not running any ads, be sure to contact them first and ask if it is okay to send them your résumé package. Otherwise, if they haven't talked to you before, it will most likely go directly into the trash.

Always know the name and correct spelling of the contact person you are sending your package to. Promise me that you will NEVER, EVER AGAIN address an application like this to "To Whom It May Concern"

Your Cover Letter and Testimonials

Mention your enclosed testimonials in your cover letter. Combine the best quotes from each testimonial you have received with any contact information for that individual. Don't go on for more than one page. When choosing clips to use, think book or movie reviews.

"…the most friendly caretaker we have ever had!"
Don Larson, Brookside Apartments, Burbank, CA

"John has been a huge asset to our team these last two years. He has single-handedly increased the profitability of our car wash! Thanks, John."
Kelly & Steve Keyes, Wash Perfect

"John took care of our team as if we were family. He truly went out of his way to make our stay enjoyable."
Dr. Alex Todd, Doctors Without Borders

Writing a Résumé That Stands Out

There are many great books on the subject of résumé writing. Over the next several pages I'll touch on broader concepts that will help you create a résumé fit for an owner or property manager.

First off, the most important part of your résumé is that you have had long-term employment—somewhere, anywhere. Next is any experience you have had managing anything or anyone. Owners and managers are looking for stability and the capability to follow through with daily or weekly tasks. They need some sense of your trustworthiness and ability to follow through.

Attach the résumé and references as unsecured Adobe .pdf & MS Word 97 .doc. You would be surprised how many companies do not update their software.

If you have no residential management experience, keep your résumé relevant to addressing your stability (the retail job you have held for the last six years), your capability to follow through and manage (your three seasons as a Little League coach) and your great customer service (your work at a phone center).

You must get out of the "me" mind-set and start to think like a property owner. What do *they* want? In the most basic sense, they want:

- Their property to be cared for
- The rent rates to be competitive
- Low or no vacancy
- Long-term residents
- Reliable, positive return on investment

When writing your résumé, address the desires above and you'll be in good shape. Other good practices are:

Keep it brief. You have less than 10 seconds to grab their attention. State your most relevant work experience first. Make it memorable and applicable to the position. Try to keep it to one page, but no longer than two. If you can't fill out a section of your résumé, don't include it. You don't want to create a subheading titled "Awards and Honors" and then put "None" underneath it.

Don't exaggerate your abilities or your work experience. Even if you get the job based on your exaggerations, you will probably be found out quickly.

Check over your spelling and grammar and get feedback. Once you have written your cover letter and résumé, get some trusted friends to go over it as well. Ask them if it they believe it is a true representation of you. Give them a deadline of 24 to 48 hours. If you are wary of doing this, that may be a sign you have inflated your actual experience.

Tailor your résumé to the position you are applying for. If they use the term "caretaker" in the advertisement, use the term "caretaker" on your résumé. You want to make yourself and your experience relevant and congruent to the position you are applying for. I'm not suggesting that you change your previous job title—just use the position poster's terminology when possible.

Let the owner/manager know you will be emailing a résumé and cover letter. Though email is significantly faster and cheaper than postal mail, a beautifully crafted résumé presented on high-quality paper carries more weight.

Call before emailing and let them know you are sending it to them. Check to see that you have the email address correct. If they want the résumé emailed, send them

Employers may Google you and find your blog or Facebook pages. Never post something online you wouldn't want them to see.

another one via snail mail the same day, as well. Follow up the next day with another phone call. The following day they should receive your paper résumé in their mailbox. At the very least, it will show that you took one step more than the other applicants. More important, it puts you at the front of their mind once again.

List places of employment, positions you have held and term of employment, but not dates. If you graduated high school in 1978—it doesn't really matter anymore. If you worked in a Wendy's drive-thru for 10 days in 1996, don't even list it. Do you really want to answer questions about that?

Include all contact info. Be sure you include your full name and all pertinent contact info at the top of the page. But don't list Facebook or your blog unless you are willing to wager your career and reputation on them.

Check email attachments. Make sure you attach your résumé and cover letter to the email before you send it off! If you haven't heard back, perhaps they weren't attached.

What Should Your Résumé Contain?

You need to include anything in your résumé that says:

- I manage projects well.
- I manage people well.
- I have pride of ownership.
- I am trusted by others.
- I am organized.
- I plan ahead and follow through.

The idea is that the owner/manager will read your résumé and want to meet you.

The idea is that the owner/manager will read your résumé and want to meet you. That is it. Your résumé is merely to get you to that next level. You may display a range of talents and qualifications that no one else has, but **having an outgoing personality and being likable may be what will land you the position in the end.**

Be sure to provide information about the following in your résumé:

- Your ability to communicate with teams and clients.
- Your "roll-up-your-sleeves" work ethic.
- Your ability to work in teams and be directed by superiors.
- Your ability to direct others and work independently.
- Your aptitude in systems, equipment and software that may pertain to managing.
- Your creativity and ingenuity.

Remember, they are not looking for someone with a master's degree in real estate. Keep it simple; if you're responding to an ad, address the ad in a point-by-point manner. Use everyday speech for on-site management positions. Don't get overly technical while describing work you have done in an industry that has nothing to do with property or people management. Overall, your résumé just needs to read well.

"I recently interviewed an individual who admitted they had no work experience, but I could see that they had a good attitude and were motivated, willing to learn, excited and outgoing. I look for these qualities above all else when choosing whom I interview.

Training a person to do something is easy; trying to motivate a lazy person or keep a person positive is much more challenging."

— Troy, Entrepreneur

And by all means, tell the truth! Don't falsify or exaggerate facts. Be creative with your writing, get input from others, and put your best-self forward. Always have someone with an objective view read it over for you before you send it.

For a thorough explanation of proper résumé layout, use this great resource from Virginia Tech: http://www.career.vt.edu/jobsearc/resumes/content.htm

I will tell you right now that merely sending owners or management companies an unsolicited résumé will get you nowhere. To them, it is another form of junk mail, simply because there is no relevant connection made between what you are asking for (by presenting your résumé) and any reference to you as a person in the real world. You and your résumé merely sit in *the paper world.* You must build a *physical connection* between your résumé and the owner or manager before you can possibly move forward. So it is vital that you introduce yourself first.

Get Testimonial-Style References

A good reference is worth more than its weight in platinum. If used correctly, it can greatly improve your chances of landing the position you seek.

What I am talking about here is a reference in testimonial form. This could also be considered a letter of recommendation by some. You are leveraging the status or authority of another outside source to build "social proof" that persuades an owner or manager you are a great person.

> **Mix it up!** *If you find that your references are more energetic, don't title the sheet, "References." Call it "Exciting Testimonials." Just think how you will stand out.*

Mix it up! If you find that your references are more energetic, don't title the sheet "References." Call it "Exciting Testimonials." Just think how you will stand out.

If over the years you collect 10, 20 or more of these in your portfolio, you will find them invaluable! You can use them to establish your reputation for quality work and integrity anywhere in the world. And the best part is, *they never become outdated!*

Get in the habit of collecting testimonials from people you work for. Scan them and collect them in a folder online. That way, if you misplace the original, you still have one you can access and print out anywhere. Once you become a Community Executive, collect testimonials from your happy residents, too.

When you're starting out with absolutely no experience managing anything, you may have to figure out how you can get some kind of relevant experience. Make it easy to start collecting references in a testimonial form. Just think how you will stand out, with your quotes and testimonials from people you have worked with. It is also much more visually impressive than the short list of names and phone numbers other applicants may present.

Here are some simple ideas to start adding powerful references to your résumé:

Ask your employer. I know many of you are cringing at this idea. But if you are good at what you do and you have an amicable relationship with your supervisor at work, tell them you are looking to become a resident manager/Community Executive and that you would appreciate a *letter of recommendation* from them specifically aimed at helping you find such a position. Assure them that you enjoy working where you do and that you have no plans to move on to a different job—you are just looking to cut your housing costs and keep your current job. Ask them to address a specific area that you believe is one of your strong points and that would impress a property owner/manager, as well. To ease their mind, have them put the term "resident manager" in the letter, so that they know you aren't using it to apply for a job with their competition. If they are still hesitant, ask if they would be willing to edit or approve and sign a recommendation you write; people do this all the time.

House-sit or dog-sit for friends going on vacation. Do it in exchange for a little money or for free, with the understanding that they will give you an honest testimonial at the end. If you did a good job watching their dog, watering the plants and shoveling the snow from their sidewalk while they were gone, ask them to put it in writing, or write something up for them and have them edit or approve and sign it.

Take in short-term roommates. Does an organization or house of worship you belong to have people visiting from out of town for a weekend or a couple of weeks? If you feel comfortable doing so, provide a place for them to stay. Let your guests know you are collecting references to improve your odds of becoming a Community Executive. If they are like most people, they will be very happy to help you out as you have just helped them.

Host couch-surfers and vagabonds. Thrifty and adventurous travelers have found a portal to save money on their rooming costs when traveling. The website couchsurfing.org has built a reputation over the last few years for connecting travelers with hosts. It is a community that fosters safety and enjoyable experiences for both parties, and using it can be a good way to collect a lot of reviews/testimonials in a couple of months.

Take on a temporary job as a resident manager. Ask neighborhood rental property owners if there is work you could do for them on a temporary basis, or if they need help with a bigger project. Every property owner needs to take a vacation, and every time they do, they need to find someone to hold down the fort in their absence. Let them know you want to become a resident manager. If you do good work, they may be more interested in telling their property-owning friends about you—or, if they are really smart, they'll offer you a position themselves.

Check with your own apartment complex. Check with the apartment complex you currently reside at to see if they have any positions available for you, or at least a small task or two you can do around the property. See if they need someone to staff the office on weekends or during an employee's absence. Get them to write a review noting your character and work ethic.

Take on roommates. Not only will roommates cut your housing cost, but by living with them, you can get experience managing people. If you can take in roommates, maintain boundaries and collect rent from them. If a roommate moves out as a friend, it's a good sign that you have a unique gift for dealing with people!

Take our class and become a Certified Community Executive. Having a certification shows that you have a measurable amount of knowledge about managing property and residents. **Certified Community Executives** also have a range of sales tools at their disposal, such as brochures and websites explaining what you are capable of offering both owners and management companies.

Here are some ideas for testimonials you could acquire that would help you prove yourself in other areas to enhance your reference sheet:

"I need more social proof that I am good at bookkeeping."

Joan just helped me file my business taxes. She is a smart cookie. She helped me organize all of my books to get my taxes in on time this year. Thanks, Joan!

Marty Smith *(your friend from college)*
123 My Street
Santa Clara, CA 95051
(555) 555-1234

"I need more social proof that I can change a light bulb."

I wanted to write a quick note about Joan. She did an amazing job installing the ceiling fan in my living room. She has also helped me unclog my garbage disposal on occasion. I can always count on Joan for her handiness!

Mrs. Eloise Day *(your elderly neighbor)*
321 My Street
Santa Clara, CA 95051
(555) 555-4321

"I need more social proof that I can maintain a property's website."

Joan is such a tech-savvy woman. She built my pet store a web page in just two days! I was able to finally give people detailed directions to my shop, put up photos of our most recent arrivals and tell customers about our special offers—all 24 hours a day. Joan also placed an area on my website where people could enter their email addresses and I could add them to my mailing list. She also made me a Facebook page! I get compliments from customers all the time now. She is a miracle worker! Thanks again! She was well worth the money.

Sandy Blue *(your mom's best friend)*
213 My Street
Santa Clara, CA 95051
(555) 555-3421

Do a little work for people you know and get them to write you a testimonial. Make it easy for them to do. Do something you are comfortable with now, or learn how to do something simple that will make you more competitive.

Additional Points to Consider

Use quality paper. When sending out a résumé package in paper form, be sure to use the highest-quality paper. Make sure all three documents (your résumé, cover letter and your references or testimonials) are printed on the same paper.

Change your voicemail. When you are seeking a resident manager position, it is important to create a simple and professional voicemail greeting. It needs to clearly identify you to callers. Remove any gimmicks or music from your greeting. Smile and say…

"You have reached Hans at (555) 222-1234. Please leave your name, phone number and message, and I will return your call as soon as possible. Thanks— have a nice day!"

Use the right formats for your email attachments. Attach your résumé and references as unsecured Adobe PDFs or in Microsoft Word 97.doc format, which nearly anyone can open. You would be surprised at how many people and companies do not update their software.

Google yourself. Employers may Google you and find your blog or Facebook pages. Never post something online you wouldn't want them to see. If you discover that you have posted such a thing, take it down.

Getting a Quality Introduction

Do you know the true power of quality introductions? It's all about leveraging the relationships you have and the ones you create. There is nothing sneaky or underhanded about it. You are simply asking a friend or acquaintance to introduce you to someone who may bring you one step closer to getting the position you set out to find.

Ask around and you will very likely find a friend or a family member who knows someone who owns rental property—it may be as easy as your sister knowing the owner of her apartment complex. Once you are introduced to the property owner, and even if they do not have a position open, ask them if they know someone who may need an employee of your caliber. Many owners are involved in associations and clubs where other residential property owners congregate.

Getting Interviewed

If you want to get interviewed by a property management company, you will first need to know:

- How to answer the advertisement
- About the property that needs resident management
- About the owner and/or management company
- How to project quality continuity on every "touch-point"
- How you will best position yourself as the best fit for the job

Know How to Answer the Advertisement

It is vital to complete your due diligence. To answer an advertisement for resident manager position with confidence, you need to do your homework and know everything you possibly can about the property and the owner or management company. You must have a plan, even if it is a simple one.

Here is where you will shine as an applicant. No one else will seem as good-looking or as prepared as you—even if you have little to no property management experience. Taking enough time to know the property and the owner or manager enough to show you actually care will help the interviewer get the feeling that you are already the resident manager and are merely reporting in for clarification. Part of this is your mind-set. You should act as though you are already the resident manager, because deep down inside you know you can do the job well and are confident that they have chosen the right person by interviewing you. Your interview with them is merely a formality.

Remember the old saying "There are no dumb questions"? Well, there are. Dumb questions are the ones whose answers can be found online or in general are obvious to people who are *capable resident managers*. These are the questions whose answers are right on the management company's website.

Only ask the questions you couldn't answer on your own with a little digging. Ask clarifying questions. Don't reiterate the ad for the interviewer. Don't ever say, "Um, it says here 'free 2-bedroom apartment'—is it nice? Does it have central air-conditioning? Does it have flush toilets?". This is not your opportunity to negotiate what you can get out of the deal. First, they have to want you.

When you make your first contact, simply say you are calling about the ad for a resident manager and ask for a time to set up an interview. Even if it does not end up being the right position for you, you will gain valuable experience. Practicing your approach and the questions you ask and learning about differing management styles will help you greatly and prepare you for the right position down the road.

Your brevity and professionalism will surprise the owner or management company right off the bat. If they say they have already narrowed down their candidates, tell them that you would still appreciate the chance to compete and ask if you can get an interview just the same. Your boldness and determination will really impress them—at least, they would impress me. Could you say no to someone so tenacious?

OPA!

When looking for the right situation, you must learn to "OPA":

- Observe
- Position
- Act

This is a three-step creative process:

- ***Observe the need*** by knowing about the property and the neighborhood.
- ***Position yourself*** as a knowledgeable and capable individual.
- ***Act quickly*** when you see an opportunity.

Positioning without observing will leave you working with too little information. It will make you seem naive and unprepared when talking with owners or managers. Know about the company, owner and property before contacting them, or you will just sound like every other salesperson who calls.

Observing and then acting will in many cases leave you unprepared as well. When you see a need or an opening, contact the owner or manager with a strategy. Once you understand the situation in more detail, you'll know what you're going to say and can write up a simple game plan. Still, don't give yourself more than 24 to 48 hours to act on an opportunity—the more practice you have, the faster you will grasp opportunities.

Worst of all is observing and positioning without acting. Nothing happens without acting. Even if you don't feel you have all the information or you haven't taken a long time to figure everything out, nothing is worse than inaction. Even if you get 99 percent of the way to accepting a resident manager position and then find out it isn't what you bargained for, you'll still have the whole experience of approaching, interviewing and negotiating the deal, which you can apply to the next opportunity.

What if you get a resident manager position and it isn't what you thought it would be? If you don't sign a long-term rental contract, you can always give notice and leave the position. I believe you should never sign a long-term lease or contract until you are firmly ensconced in a community you actually love. At the same time, get out there and get some experience before you quit every position just because it isn't *perfect*.

Get your name out there. Aim high. After making contact with an owner or management company, keep in touch with them. Staying fresh in the minds of owners or management companies serves you well in the long run.

Answering the Ad

Remember: The idea here is to have positioned yourself correctly by knowing what you are getting into. Have your résumé, cover letter, references and business cards ready, in case they want to book an appointment or informal interview the same day you contact them.

Calling about the job listing: Call the number and talk to someone about the position. Have your list of questions prepared ahead of time; if they have time to speak with you, be ready to ask the questions. Keep in mind that they may have questions for you—be sure to have answers prepared for the most common questions employers ask (see Chapter 7).

Voicemail: Many times when you call a small company or an individual owner, you'll just get their voicemail. If you reach an answering machine with a general greeting, leave a simple message. Remember to smile while you speak. They will hear it in your voice. Say:

"Hello, my name is [*first name only*], and I'm inquiring about the resident manager position listed [*in the newspaper, on craigslist, etc.*]. I would really appreciate a call back so we could briefly discuss the opening. You may reach me any time on my personal cell phone at area code [*xxx*], [*xxx-xxxx*]. Again that is area code [*xxx*], [*xxx-xxxx*]. Thank you! I look forward to hearing from you soon."

Sending a fax: Be sure to do some research on the fax number first. In other words, don't fax a cover letter and résumé blindly. The more you know about the company, the more you can tailor your letter and résumé to the position. When you respond by fax, you will want to send your cover letter first, followed by your résumé and then your testimonial-style references.

Stopping by: If you stop by to visit the owner or management company in person, don't make it a lengthy affair. They are busy; you should seem too busy to chitchat as well. You can find out more about the opening later, at the interview. If you do have to ask a question, it should only be to get you enough information to continue your investigative work. For example, if the ad doesn't state the property's location, ask, so you can take a look at it before a possible interview.

If it turns out the place is a real dive, *don't cancel the interview*. I suggest that you still go through with it for the experience alone. Realize that the owner or company may have other properties or positions they feel you're a better fit for. If you are offered a job you don't want, you can always say thank you and politely turn it down. You may ask that they keep you in mind for other positions that open up that are more like what you desire.

Know About the Property That Needs Resident Management

Deciphering the Advertisement With a Little Investigative Work

Sometimes an ad can be vague at best. When it comes to location, the more you know, the better you will be prepared for an interview. You will first want to determine if you are comfortable with the safety of the property location. Don't bother with unsafe or even borderline areas. There are a lot of positions you could get tomorrow—but you may not *want* the ones you could get tomorrow.

You will find that the biggest problem with being a Community Executive is picking the wrong property to manage—period; end of story. However, you can find out

> *The biggest problem with being a Community Executive is picking the wrong property to manage—period; end of story.*

where a property is located with a few simple tools and techniques. To learn more about how, go to **www.CommExAcademy.com/findprop.**

Getting to Know the Property Quickly

Once you have scoped out a property's location using maps.google.com, become a Junior Private Investigator and do the following:

1. Drive right by the property. Was it easy to find? Does it stand out from the others? Is it labeled on a sign?

2. Note the first things that stand out as you drive by. Curb appeal is one of the biggest selling points of a property. If a prospective resident pulls up to the property and is turned off by run-down buildings, trash on the grounds, dead grass, political banners and the like, you may have a hard sell. At least you'll know what to change with your fresh eyes.

3. Walk around as much of the property as you can, if you feel it is safe. You will want to make notes of all of the things that you notice. Also, note everything you believe you could improve. Very few people who get the interview will know anything about the owner or the company and, strangely enough, will know little to nothing about the property they are hoping to manage. Ask yourself:
   - Can I have a positive impact on the property as Community Executive?
   - Do I feel that the neighborhood is safe?
   - Would I be able to fill the units using my creativity and professionalism?

   Note the landscaping and condition of the exterior of the buildings. Are there problems with erosion of the landscaping? Are downspouts detached causing a wet basement? Can you give the place a face-lift by:
   - updating a few light fixtures?
   - replacing the unit address numbers?
   - renewing door hardware?
   - adding a fresh coat of paint to the doors and trim?
   - giving the property a name?
   - putting up a high-quality, low-cost permanent sign?

4. Approach residents and ask them:
   - *Is there an on-site manager?*
   - *What is the management like?*
   - *How do you like living here?*
   - *How long have you lived here?*
   - *Do you feel safe here?*

You can tell them that you are considering at moving to the property and that you are trying to get a feel for it and the neighborhood. It is amazing what we have found out about a property by talking to the people who live there, as well as next-door neighbors.

Neighbors can be your best resource. They are happy to tell you all of the problems they have had with the property in question and if the neighborhood is on the decline or the rise. They will tell you if it is a great place to live or if it is party central. They will tell you all about the crime in the neighborhood, whom they don't like and who has the big dog that barks at one o'clock in the morning.

Mentally note the positive and negative. Get the names of the people you talk to. The best way to do this is to give them your name first, after you have been talking to them for a couple minutes and have established a rapport. If you give them your full name, usually people will reciprocate with their full name. Remember it and write it down later. You will refer to these people during your interview. **This is a _huge advantage to_ you!**

Don't tell residents or neighbors that you are applying for the resident manager position—it may not be public knowledge yet. Doing so may stir up conflict within the community.

Know About the Owner

You can learn who owns a property simply by going to your city or county's property assessor's website. If your query result is an LLC, do what you can and investigate the name of the corporation or the billing address on file. Type in the address of the property and view the ownership history. From there, you can search the name of the owner and find out where they live and how long they have owned the property.

In most cases, the longer they have owned the property, the more sophisticated the investor and the higher the possibility that they have money to make improvements. Why? you ask. Because they have probably paid off most of the property if they have owned it for decades.

Even if they are highly leveraged with the property, sophisticated investors have other properties that they can shift monies to and from. They are more willing to put money into the property if you can convince them it will increase revenue.

The flip side of this equation is that new owners are generally less experienced investors and may not have as much cash to invest into the property. They may be highly leveraged and running on a tiny budget, or strictly looking at numbers and not at property condition. This is not always true, but in many cases, it is.

Know About the Property Management Company

Find the name of the management company by doing a reverse phone search or by searching under the property address. Sometimes it is listed right on the rental sign. Once you find the website, read the entire site. Know who the founder, principal and property managers are. Know what their motto, mission statement and taglines are.

Know their colors, read their testimonials, know their staff and what positions they hold. Photos of staff are even better. Some sites go into great lengths about the personalities behind the company, while others hide even the names of the staff. What could this tell you? Perhaps one easy-going company has more of a family-like atmosphere, while the other maintains a high-stress work environment that leads to high employee turnover.

By going through this investigation, you are showing the owner or management company that you care. It may be enough just to know—you don't have to get all creepy by telling them everything about everyone who works there and the funny things you saw on their personal Facebook pages. You are merely collecting as much information as you can about the opportunity at hand. You are also familiarizing yourself with the company. It will be as if you have already walked into the management office and met everyone.

At this point, you will be ready to walk into the interview with your eyes wide open—ready to dazzle and amaze. Be confident that you know the property, the recommendations you will make, who the owner or manager is, the neighborhood and what your role will be as resident manager. You are the professional they have been looking for. And just because you make suggestions doesn't mean you will be handling all of them yourself. You are simply showing the owner or company that you care about their investment and that you can see how a few inexpensive updates will give the property a fresh look that they may or may not know it needs.

Once you complete one of these surveys of the property and personnel, you can create a "swipe file." A swipe file is a folder you keep files of ideas you have, great ads you have seen, helpful articles and other content you can pull out later. This file will serve as a shortcut to remind you later of all the relevant material that came from your first or second property review.

How to Display Quality Across All "Touch-Points"

Your image is the combination of experiences that people have had with you through each *touch-point*. Your touch-points are your business card, résumé, the voicemail you left, your clothing, perfume, Facebook page, the quality of your voice—they are *you, the whole package.*

When you visit an owner or management company in person, you must have your game on. Be prepared to be interviewed right there and then. It's always possible that the receptionist will direct you to a manager who just happens to have a few minutes to meet with you.

First off, you have to show up when they are in a good mood and not overly busy. Always visit a management company's office between Tuesday and Thursday, from 10 a.m. to 3 p.m. Don't go on Mondays or Fridays. On Monday, the staff will be checking through messages from the weekend and handling work orders having to do with those messages. On Friday, everyone will be thinking about the weekend, or key staff may be out. Don't visit on those days—you'll just be getting in the way, and that is not going to leave a good impression.

Don't go during Saturday or Sunday office hours, either. Weekend workers are generally trained to show units and set up appointments for showings during the workweek. They may not even know what to do with your résumé.

Also, don't go on the first or last day of any month. This is when the bulk of rent checks come in and when bills are due. The office staff will be very busy with additional paperwork on top of the normal phone calls and showings these days. Only go if you are trying to meet their deadline for accepting applications, and then be brief. Staying and asking them questions about the position may only annoy them.

Preparation

Be confident and know what you want to say. Prepare ahead of time with a couple questions you are curious about and bring along your résumé package.

Ask whom you should talk to about any available positions. If they do not have any positions available, ask if it is okay to check in with them later to see if anything has changed. If they say yes, put a recurring appointment on your calendar to call them once a month, like clockwork. This tells them that you are not only persistent, but reliable, consistent and well organized. Note the name of the staff you talk to, as well as the human resources or hiring manager.

Be sure to contact 15 to 20 places you are interested in. The more contacts you have, the better a position you are in. You may run into multiple offers at some point. Don't hold on to one lead for a month just because you think it will be a great position. The owner or company may already have other managers in mind for it, or the deal they may offer you may not be all that great. The best practice is to keep in contact with several options simultaneously.

Owners and management companies are looking for stability. They don't want to have to train and retrain people. They, like you, want to "set it and forget it" as much as possible. Mention to them that you are looking for a long-term position.

AVAILABLE TO READERS ONLY
Bonus article *"If all else fails, **this will work**:"*
Email bonus1@CommExAcademy.com

Chapter 7

THE INTERVIEW: PUTTING YOUR BEST SELF FORWARD

Most experienced owners and managers can tell if you will be a good fit for them within about 30 seconds to one minute. It all comes down to how you present yourself and how confident you seem about what you say and how you act. They are looking at your physical appearance, listening to your vocal qualities and vocabulary, and assessing your attitude and overall level of professionalism. They want someone with stability and confidence, someone who can be friendly but who can also lay down the law when necessary.

In most cases, they are not looking for a sweet, flowery, people-pleasing pushover. Residents will run all over a passive manager. Nor are they looking for a hard-nosed, club-wielding security guard. (If the property is in a rough neighborhood, and that *is* what they want, look elsewhere.) Be yourself—but be your best, prepared self.

If you stop in to their office twice wearing a suit and tie, and then once on your way to the gym in shorts and a T-shirt, they will wonder who the real you is. You need to display a consistent *personal brand* to build credibility and integrity. When they think of you, professionalism, courtesy and confidence should come to mind.

Preparing For the Interview Questions

You've already done all of the necessary research to become knowledgeable about the property, residents, owner and management company. Now you need to be ready for the questions that may come your way.

Role-play with a friend and answer the following questions (without laughing):

"Tell me a little about yourself." Don't go into a long diatribe. Give them the highlights of your relevant experience.

"What makes you qualified to manage our property?" If you have no management experience, tell them how your past experience has given you insight into how to manage people, keep books, sell, provide great customer service, etc.

"Why do you want to be our resident manager?" You like the property, and you talked to some of the residents and they seem very nice. It is a great location, the responsibilities fit your abilities well, and you really like the idea of reduced or free rent.

"When was a time you demonstrated leadership?" You coached Little League, organized a fund-raiser or managed seven cashiers during the chaos of the Christmas season.

"What do you know about our company?" Tell them everything you know about them. You've done your homework, now answer the question.

"Tell me about a time in the past when you resolved a dispute." Be specific. Find an instance where both sides felt like they won the argument, or were at least satisfied.

"Tell me about a time you worked under tremendous pressure." Tell them about when you finished a massive amount of work in with a little time to do it or how you handled an emergency.

"How would you be an asset to our company?" Your job is to protect and grow the owner's investment. Let them know that your first job is to improve cash flow by renting out any vacant units as quickly as humanly

possible. Also let them know that you are a stickler for timely maintenance and that your job is to make sure the residents remain satisfied.

"What is your greatest strength?" Setting up efficient systems for managing people and rental property.

"Tell me about your management style." Your approach should be to actually manage projects and people, not to be a property babysitter. You like an efficiently run property. You like systems, following the methods that work and replacing those that fall short.

"What is your greatest weakness?" Be honest, and don't say that you work too hard.

"What questions do you have for me?" **This is the most important question.** Ask them: In a perfect world, what does the ideal resident manager look like to you?

What to Wear to the Interview

For men, attire should be "workday casual": nice, newer jeans or khakis and a collared pique/golf shirt or a long-sleeve, solid-color cotton shirt—all wrinkle-free. A great way to find out how the men who already work for the company dress is to check for photos of staff on their website. However, if they really dress down (in worn jeans, for example), then at least wear new pressed jeans or khakis. Otherwise, you'll look like you aren't even trying to look nice for your interview.

A great way to find out how they dress is by checking for photos of staff on their website. However, if they really dress down (in worn jeans, for example), then at least wear pressed jeans or khakis. Otherwise, you'll look like you aren't even trying to look nice for your interview.

Have a clean-shaven face, be showered, and remove piercings. If you have tattoos, cover them if it's easy enough to do. You may think I'm being a prude, but you will be judged by your appearance in about two seconds. Why would you do anything that could make getting the position any harder?

For women, that means a conservative dress or dress slacks and a conservative blouse or shirt. Don't let the women in the office talk about how high your skirt was or how low your V-neck was. Going in conservative will help you fit in without sparking cattiness in the office before you're even interviewed. And don't go for sexy! Let your first impression be your personality, not what you're wearing.

I'm not saying that you have to leave the real you behind—you just need to fit into the mold of what the owner or company are already most familiar with. It is all about that first impression—followed by every impression that comes after. You could have a full, relevant résumé and a fantastic personality, but if you show up to the office with a lip ring and tattoos of skulls and flames on your forearms from a decade ago, and smell like an ashtray, you will have a much harder time convincing the company or owner that you are a professional who can take care of their investment.

Be the Manager in *Your Mind* First

You have to be the manager in *your mind* before an owner or company will see you as management material. Stand up straight. Sit up straight. Be friendly and alert. The funny thing is, if you have confidence in yourself and the ability to do the job well, you are 75 percent of the way there.

Dress as they do. When you do, they will immediately feel a connection with you, before you even open your mouth. They will subconsciously be thinking, "Hey, he's like me. He understands how we do things around here." And that is exactly what you want.

The Interview

Here are a few things to keep in mind while in the interview:

Be relaxed. Center yourself and picture a positive outcome. Oddly enough, you *can* be both energetic and relaxed. If you are feeling nervous—if you find yourself thinking, "I'm nervous about this interview"—then change it into excitement. Say to yourself, "I'm excited about this interview."

Be prepared. Know your answers to the most common questions (above). Know about the owner, company and the property ahead of time. If you have done the research, simply put it to use.

Be professional. Wear the proper attire for the occasion and demonstrate common courtesy.

Be mindful of your body language. Sit up straight. Watch for your "poker tells." Don't fidget, tap, kick your leg, turn your ring or cross your arms or legs. Touching your face tells an interviewer that you may be trying to hide something. Touching your head can signify that you are unsure.

Maintain eye contact. Don't look away when you're answering a question. Look people in the eye for at least 10 seconds, or mirror what they do. When you look away, it seems as though you are hiding something. Hold as much eye contact as they do.

Be creative. Have some free or inexpensive ideas that could improve the property. To be even more creative, say that you would be happy to manage those projects from bid collection to completion.

The interview starts with your first contact and continues until the end of any probationary period. During that time, you may be in the position to negotiate. That is what we'll cover next.

Chapter 8

THE ART OF THE DEAL: NEGOTIATING EXACTLY WHAT YOU WANT

Your happiness over the next several months hinges on your ability to negotiate the arrangements of your new position. If you don't want to sign up to become an indentured servant for the next year or more, you need to do your homework. This guide will help you navigate the initial negotiation of your work-in-trade agreement. Know that many owners or property managers want to get a resident manager for the lowest cost possible, while others are generous and just happy to have someone of your caliber apply. It is crucial that you know both what you want and what you will not agree to.

For starters, you need to have done your homework before your negotiation meeting. Be prepared, because negotiations may occur during the first interview. If the owner or property manager has been interviewing several candidates, it is possible that they will be ready to hire on the spot. If they recognize you as a reliable and professional applicant, things may progress quickly to "When can you start?"

Things to Keep In Mind When Negotiating

Know what the owner/manager needs or wants. They are all about *"What's in it for me?"* What are they really concerned about? Keep in mind that in general property owners and management companies want:

- Their property to be cared for
- The rent rates to be competitive
- Low or no vacancy
- Long-term residents
- A reliable, positive return on investment

If you can address how you will efficiently handle their concerns, they are more apt to go with you.

Go into negotiations with an "abundance" mind-set. This may sound a little counterintuitive, but if you go into negotiations thinking "What can I offer *them*?" you will win them over. Once you know what they want and show them how you can deliver it—as well as how you bring additional skills to the table—they will choose you over Joe Shmo.

Make it a win-win. They may have wanted a 24-hour, on-call maintenance person. You can respond to that if you have already received quotes from nearby handymen who would be willing to work on a per-visit or hourly basis at $30 an hour. The owner may have wanted someone to hold daily office hours, but that may be because no one has ever been able to keep the property near 100 percent occupancy, like you will.

Every time you see a duty you really don't want to do or feel unqualified for, be sure to present them with low-cost alternatives that are actually more attractive for them. To have a handyman on call at $30 an hour is worth it. Most resident managers will end up calling a contractor in for emergency maintenance for double that rate. If there is any question in your mind about who would pay for a service, it is the owner, not you.

Add value. Offer to do things that you know will add value to a property that will take you little time (e.g., planting flowers in spring, cleaning out basement, setting up and maintaining the property website or blog). Many bigger tasks could be one-time or seasonal or otherwise rarely need doing. Mention a seasonal task that is coming up. Why? Because it is on the top of their mind, and it shows it is on the top of yours, too.

Reiterate what they are asking you to do. "So when you say you want me to rent apartments, you are saying I would be placing ads on craigslist every Friday, answering calls, booking appointments, notifying residents of entry, showing apartments, sending applications to the main office and signing leases with new residents. Is that correct?"

Know what you want to get out of it. What is your time worth? If the owner/manager wants you to do a laundry list of duties that will take you 20 hours to complete in a month, and the credit is $200, is $10 an hour worth your time? Would $400 a month in credit or $20 an hour be worth your time? Could you see streamlining the tasks in the near future?

Know which tasks are everyday duties and which are paid per hour. Remember, the more you make per hour, the faster you will be debt free and have a growing investment portfolio.

Know what you can streamline. If the owner/manager asks that the resident manager hold office hours for a 34-unit complex from 9 a.m. to 3 p.m., Monday through Saturday, they really may be saying, "We want to know that residents can contact the resident manager easily, and that prospects can stop in and check out apartments when necessary." Many of those concerns could be easily handled with a cell phone, email address and a thorough website.

Do they have other tasks they are willing to pay you for? Painting, cleaning units, planting flowers, etc. And if so, are you even willing to do them, or would you rather hire them out?

Get it in writing. Make sure that all your responsibilities and the compensation for them are written out and signed off on by you and the proper representative of the property. If you don't, you may experience "responsibility creep." Once the manager sees how you have streamlined the operation of the property, they may feel you need to stay busier. If your resident manager duties were never written down, they may ask you to start painting the units, to clean out the basement, to install new windows or to run to the bank for them, and on and on.

Sign a month-to-month lease. Don't tie yourself into a yearlong lease! Don't get stuck in a bad situation. The best-case scenario is for you to be able give an owner or manager a 30-day written notice that you are leaving your position, and for them to have to give you a 60-day written notice of termination. As a courtesy, staying on for a full 60 days after you given notice will help them find someone for you to train.

Define all responsibilities clearly. Don't sign anything with responsibilities described in an open-ended fashion, like:

Shovel snow
Rent out all units—whatever it takes
Turn over units

Ambiguous responsibilities can mean just about anything down the road. Make sure that you and the owner have the same definition as to the scope of each duty. If they say, "Make sure the front walk is free of ice and snow" or "Test the four fire alarms once a month," you know exactly what they mean.

Negotiate benefits that will help you do your job better. Such benefits might include a landline phone, a cell phone (a prepaid Net10 or TracPhone), Internet access for updating the website and answering emails, a fax machine for faxing applications to the main office, office supplies, tools for work, parking, electricity, heat and updates to your apartment. Some things you will be able to negotiate for later, after you have proven yourself.

Know your ceiling. Don't ask for too much—they may pull away the offer from you. Get a feel for the interviewer by watching their body language. Don't demand everything; just figure out what their base is and work up from that.

Understand marketing. Know how you can improve the owner's or company's marketing to get more leads. Look at what they are doing and ask how they think the results have been. (More on that in chapter 12.)

Know your hours. How many hours do you want to work as a Community Executive? <u>Don't tell them you plan on working an hour or two a week.</u>

Your thought process should NOT be, *How do I fill 20 hours a week managing a property?* It should be, *How efficient can I be while completing all the required duties with excellence?* Just because the last resident manager had nothing better to do than walk the property six days a week jingling a big ring of keys in his hand, that doesn't mean you have to follow suit.

> *Your thought process should NOT be, How do I fill 20 hours a week managing a property? **It should be,** How efficient can I be while completing all the required duties with excellence?*

Remember, it will take more hours up front to get things up to speed. The owner probably doesn't care how long it takes you to do your work, as long as everything is done and done well.

Know the value of your hour. Dollars per hour can be negotiated. If you work fast, tell them you are a fast worker and that you would like to receive a little more money for the work or to be paid per job. But be sure to protect yourself if you work on a pay-per-job basis. For example, they might offer to pay you $60 for each turnover, and you may take three hours to do some and 16 hours for others. When a resident leaves a lot of furniture, stains or holes in the walls, you could be in for a real treat!

Negotiate down rent. If they won't take more off your rent, negotiate additional work for pay.

Fiona and I negotiated to pay $100 rent for every vacant unit in our complex, up to $500 a month. So with every vacancy we filled, we received another $100 off rent that

> *In the six years we've been here, we've paid a total of about $400!*

month. In the six years we've been here, we've paid a total of about $400! If we lease an apartment and the owner lets the resident out of the lease early, we are not liable to pay $100 a month for the vacancy. We still need to re-rent it and we do so rapidly, but we are not penalized for the time it takes.

Get move-in time. Ask for one to two weeks to move in and get set up before starting management duties.

Helpful Phrases

- "I take pride in what I do. The condition of the property is a reflection of who I am."
- "I'm someone who is going to care for your property because I live there and it is in my best interest to keep it looking great and functioning smoothly."
- "My experience in x will help you y this property better."
- "I'm honest and dependable."
- "You can count on me to follow through."

Your List of Requests

Here is a short list of the possibilities. This is a list only limited by your creativity.

- ❐ Free housing (no rent)
- ❐ Reduced rent or rent on a sliding scale. This is what we negotiated for ourselves. Here's how it works:
    - ❐ If there are five or more vacancies in the property, your rent is $500. ($500 is our cap—our rent doesn't get higher if there are more vacancies.)
    - ❐ At four vacancies, your rent is $400. And so on—the rent drops $100 with every vacancy you fill.
    - ❐ If there are no vacancies, your rent is free.

- ❐ Free phone, if you must use the phone for business. The bill should go directly to the manager/owner. Don't be calling Thailand or London on this line without a prepaid phone card!
- ❐ Free parking. (Don't have a car? Hmmm—maybe rent your parking space or garage to someone else at a profit?)
- ❐ Free Internet, if you have to answer email inquiries or update the property website
- ❐ Free electricity
- ❐ Free gas
- ❐ Free water/sewer
- ❐ Free trash removal
- ❐ Free use of the clubhouse, pool, business center and gym
- ❐ Free use of maintenance's wood shop
- ❐ Free extra storage locker or storage shed
- ❐ Free extra parking for a second car

We have received all of the above during our tenure as managers.

What else can you think of?

_____

_____

_____

_____

_____

Make each *request* a "win-win" for you and the owner. Chances are, some things will cost them nothing (such as parking) or much less than what they charge residents. Giving you a $1,000 apartment doesn't mean they are losing $1,000 a month; their actual cost may be half that or lower. There may be tax benefits for the owner if you occupy a unit, too.

Having an on-site manager is a big bonus for the owner, management company, residents and prospective residents. And if you stay for several years, they are saving thousands of dollars on turnover costs.

Work-in-Trade Ideas

The owner or management company may ask for you to perform a few duties for, say, $300 off of your rent. Ask if they are open to expanding on that idea and including other responsibilities for additional credit. Think about the following list and check off every duty that you would feel comfortable performing. Be realistic about how much time per week it will take you to perform them. Offer to do it on a trial basis.

When you check out the property before the interview, size it up and overestimate the time your potential duties will take you. I'll show you in Chapter 11 how to streamline, outsource and batch tasks to save hours of work every week. That is the beauty of this system.

Check the items you would be willing to do or learn in exchange for totally free housing.

Administrative
- ❒ Answer and return phone calls
- ❒ Set up appointments
- ❒ Show apartments
- ❒ Process applications
- ❒ Run credit reports
- ❒ Float—show neighboring property's units
- ❒ Keep in touch with residents
- ❒ Hold office hours
- ❒ Bake cookies and make coffee for office
- ❒ Ticket cars violating parking rules
- ❒ Answer forwarded main office phone for the weekend
- ❒ Clean office
- ❒ Create flyers
- ❒ Create/manage website

- [ ] Place ads on craigslist
- [ ] Post notices
- [ ] Deposit vending machine cash into bank
- [ ] _____
- [ ] _____
- [ ] _____
- [ ] _____

Maintenance, Grounds and Cleaning

- [ ] Contact vendors and contractors
- [ ] Vacuum common areas
- [ ] Clean hallways
- [ ] Wipe down laundry rooms
- [ ] Sweep common areas
- [ ] Clean clubhouse
- [ ] Dust and dust mop
- [ ] Wet mop or wax floors
- [ ] Stock vending machine
- [ ] Change out air fresheners
- [ ] Change out burnt light bulbs
- [ ] Sweep sidewalks
- [ ] Mow lawn
- [ ] Water plants
- [ ] Pick up litter on the grounds
- [ ] Clean up parking areas
- [ ] Clean pool
- [ ] Wash windows
- [ ] Empty trash in common areas
- [ ] Perform simple maintenance
- [ ] 24-hour lock-out service
- [ ] Salt icy walkways
- [ ] Plant flowers
- [ ] Trim bushes
- [ ] Test fire alarms

- ❑ _____
- ❑ _____
- ❑ _____
- ❑ _____

Other

- ❑ Be available for additional work for pay
- ❑ Show your unit as a model
- ❑ Perform a detailed inspection of the property every __ months with a written report
- ❑ _____
- ❑ _____
- ❑ _____

Advanced work that may require additional training or certification

- ❑ Speak a second language
- ❑ Professional landscaping
- ❑ 24-hour maintenance
- ❑ Online marketing
- ❑ Receive resident payments
- ❑ Deposit resident payments
- ❑ Run profit-and-loss statements
- ❑ Sign resident leases as representative of owner[10]
- ❑ Set up property in QuickBooks Financial Software
- ❑ Archive old documents
- ❑ _____
- ❑ _____
- ❑ _____

The End Goal – *Better-Than-FREE Housing and Benefits*

Fantastic—you've done it. You've landed a position where you put in a couple hours a week and in return net *free* housing. That is your end goal in this process. If the deal you negotiate turns out to get you $500 off rent, that

---

10 This may require a real estate broker license.

is great! Just know that if you pay something for your housing, then as rent rises for the residents, so it could for you, too.

Make your end goal *better-than-free housing* because that is *exactly what it is.* It is the best-case scenario if you need a place to live.

I consider Community Executive housing better-than-free because:

- if your refrigerator breaks—you pay nothing
- as property taxes go up—you pay nothing more
- when your home needs a new roof—you're out nothing
- when the housing market crashes—you lose nothing
- if the location of your day job changes—you make a quick exit and owe nothing
- when you see an investment opportunity, be it assets to add to your bank account or an investment of time into your family—you are completely free to run with it
- your other full- or part-time job income goes two to three times as far
- **if you do your job right—you owe nothing to anyone**

All because you pay nothing for housing. You now see the full value of having free housing.

The Candid Conversation You Must Have

AFTER you accept the position as resident manager and have worked out the terms, be sure to have a candid conversation with the owner. Ask them straight out if they have any intentions to sell the property in the future.

If they say, "Possibly, down the line," tell them, "I would just appreciate it if you would let me know ahead of time, so I can best prepare in the event that my position would change or end—is that fair?"

When we have managed properties, we've seen (and distributed) a notice to residents that says something like, "*The insurance adjuster (inspector, owner, bank, etc.) will be entering your unit on this date and time to do a routine inspection...*" In most instances that is code for, "*Someone has made an offer on the property, and we've accepted their offer; however it's contingent on inspecting every unit on this date and time..."*

So just ask for the owner to be forthright with you in the event that they intend to put the property on the market. Let them know that you understand the sensitivity of such information and that you would keep it private. *The reason I say this* is because of the one time we didn't have this candid conversation with an owner. We were not prepared to leave our position when the property was sold to a developer with his own management company.

DOING
THE WORK

Chapter 9

THE 12 KEYS TO KEEPING YOUR POSITION FOREVER (AND HOW TO LOSE IT!)

There are *12 keys to keeping your position as a Community Executive forever.* I call them "keys" because having a firm grasp on them will allow you to go wherever you desire without encountering the *locked doors* that many resident managers do. By adhering to the principles set forth here, you will truly have a successful tenure as a Community Executive.

1. Your responsibilities come first. Your freedom comes second.

This is a job, not a hobby. To be a Community Executive, you need to live up to everything you committed to when you accepted the position. This system is not a way to get out of doing what you agreed to, but rather a system that allows you to do much more in a fraction of the time by working smarter. As author and speaker Tim Ferriss says, "Busywork is another form of laziness."

I know several property managers, and as one myself, I want to make sure that whoever we hire as a Community Executive does their job per our initial agreement and does it well. The terms agreed upon when you accepted the position were not just suggestions—they are part of a contract. It doesn't matter if they were written down, part of an oral agreement or sealed by a handshake. You must take responsibility to do your part *or more*. For you to receive free rent and phone, for instance, you need to provide a value of $800, $1,200 or $2,000 per month to the owner. If she doesn't see you as a great return on her investment based on the results you produce, she may need to make an adjustment: You'll do more work, you'll receive fewer benefits, or she'll find someone else.

2. You are a time manager, a people manager and an investment manager.

A Community Executive is a *time manager*. If you can handle your time well, everything else will come more easily. You will learn to plan your day's, week's, month's and year's activities in advance. You will need to separate your time between "on duty" and "off duty" to maintain your professionalism, as well as your sanity. Setting aside time to return calls, answer calls, sweep common areas, take out the trash and so forth will allow you to keep ahead of your duties while working efficiently by ***blocking time into chunks*** of work.

Many resident managers lose by removing the boundaries between their work and home life. They answer every phone call, do a little work here and there, never get to things they don't enjoy doing and pretty much run the property in a disorganized manner. Even though my natural tendency is to be disorganized, I don't *work* that way. You can't—otherwise, time will get away from you, and tasks will not get completed.

A Community Executive is a *people manager*. Sometimes it can seem like you are a social worker. Residents may come to you with their money problems, roommate problems, marriage problems and health problems. If that is happening, you have to stop and *DTR* (define the relationship). It is up to you as manager how you want to handle your relationships with residents.

You don't want to close the door on them, be terse or unfeeling, or neglect them. Show compassion and friendliness, but also adhere to the rules of the community and the lease agreement they signed. You must learn how to establish your residents' expectations about when and how you will be available to them. You'll learn to develop boundaries that will help you maintain your mental health and avoid burnout, as so many property managers and resident managers do who don't adhere to an effective system. Manage the people well, and you can avoid burnout.

A Community Executive is an *investment manager.* No oversize, walnut executive desk needed. We're not talking stocks or bonds here; in this case the investment is not only the tangible real estate, but also a living, breathing, cash-flowing business. There are costs, and there is income. The more you can decrease the costs to the owner, while maintaining or improving the community and thus increasing cash flow, the better off she and you will be.

> *Treat your residents well, and you'll have a home that won't cost you anything for many years.*

Who gets rid of an investment manager who is improving their investments every year? Nobody! Increasing the perceived value of the physical property and the amount of rent that is collected will reflect the real value of the property to the owner and to a bank. In other words, the more rental income collected, the higher the property value can be. The higher the value, the more a bank may lend to the owner to buy more property or improve the property you are managing.

The buildings must be kept up, and the grounds must remain neat and clean. Plumbing, HVAC and electrical must also function at 100 percent, 365 days a year. You are the front line. It comes down to you to make sure the investment is protected. Your "team" in keeping the investment at 100 percent is composed of your maintenance staff, the management company (if there is one) and outside contractors who do everything you or maintenance cannot. You'll help identify problems, write up detailed and effective work orders and give the owner or management company a heads-up on any areas of the property that may need to be addressed immediately or in the near future.

3.   Happy, well-behaved residents are your insurance policy.

Treat your residents well, and you'll have a home that won't cost you anything for many years. Relationships take time to develop. Don't feel discouraged if everyone doesn't love you on day one—or even year one. You are the new sheriff in town, and it may take a bit of time for people to warm up to you.

When you go out of your way for a resident and they are appreciative of your efforts, and you feel it is appropriate, ask them for help. Let them know you would deeply value a positive note that may help you in the future.

Residents don't know if you are going to be just like the last fellow the management company hired, who couldn't hack it. They may test you to see what they can get away with—be it leaving full garbage bags outside their door, parking in no-parking zones or having a loud party late into the night. Be friendly and trustworthy and follow through on what you say, and over time you will gain their trust. The longer a resident stays, the more time you save by not having to place advertisements, take and return phone calls and schedule showings and turn-over. If a resident renews their lease, there are no turn-over costs (i.e., cleaning, painting, maintenance, carpets, etc.), which alone can run into the thousands of dollars. Plus, for every month a vacated unit stays open, you add another $1,000 (or however much) to the owner's losses!

4.   The community's quality of life MUST IMPROVE.

If you don't improve the status quo by merely being there, you aren't doing your job. Because that is the exact reason you were hired—the state of the community or building wasn't up to the level of quality the owner or management company desired, so they decided to make a change. Don't take the *systematizing* of the job to mean that you don't have to do any work. In Chapter 11, we'll cover *front-loading* and how putting 100 percent effort forth in the beginning can decrease your workload 70 to 85 percent later on.

There are simple things you can do to show residents you care. If you do your job well, or remember birthdays, the names of their children or something they told you last time you talked, they will know you care. It is okay to be a friend to residents. We're all human. You're not a cowboy herding cattle. Interaction is fine—just know where to draw the line.

5. Set the tone up front.

Even if you think you know it all or you have been a manager or property manager in the past, become a student of the community. You're the new kid on the block, and you have to earn the respect of the community. So don't come in on day one standing on a milk crate with a megaphone in hand, throwing out a bunch of new rules, changes, signs or newsletters like you know the residents and their needs.

After you move in, you'll want to knock on doors and greet everyone. Keyword: humility. Residents will be much more forgiving of someone who may not know everything in the beginning but who is a hard worker and friendly.

You'll spend the first week or so working in the background; setting up systems and getting to know the needs of the community before making or suggesting any changes. Don't set up a bunch of rules that you think are necessary. Find out what the community wants, and enforcement of the rules will become much easier.

6. Know when to stick to rules.

Ordinances, agreements and rental provisions are there for a reason. If there are cars with flat tires in the parking lot that haven't moved in three months, get them moved. If music is blasting out of an apartment at midnight, knock on the door and tell them to turn it down, or call the police and have them handle it. Give residents a verbal warning and follow it up with a written notice if necessary.

If rent is due on the 1st of the month, but a resident always gets paid on the 5th, don't be a jerk and charge them late fees every month because of his employer. Talk to management and see if an exception can be made. There are good reasons to make exceptions to a rule if it makes sense. It will go a long way in building not only rapport but loyalty to the community, as well.

When you go out of your way for a resident and they are appreciative of your efforts, and you feel it is appropriate, ask *them* for help. Let them know you would deeply value a positive note that might help you in the future.

7. Maintain open communication *with boundaries.*

I've said it before: You need to set up boundaries; otherwise, you will go crazy. It is hard to feel at peace knowing that someone could stop by at any time to tell you about their problems. You will get burned out if people have an all-access pass to you and your family.

After a few days, you'll find out when people are home and usually need help. You'll see trends—when you tend to get the most calls or visits. And if you hold a job off-site, you'll obviously need to work around those hours.

We have a policy of *Call first, unless it's an emergency or you're locked out.* We've had people just open our front door and walk in, thinking that if the door was unlocked, they could enter. We quickly put a stop to that. If people know you are available every time they see a light on, they will take advantage of it.

One of the ways to foster a positive relationship with your residents is with great communication. Communicate well with residents *now* to avoid unhappiness or hard feelings *later.*

8. Keep tabs on maintenance.

Most generalized complaints about an apartment community stem from poorly handled maintenance—all you have to do is look at apartment review sites to see this. We saw one review online that said that it had taken over a week for a new water heater to be replaced and that there were bugs in the apartment. After you receive a maintenance request, you write it up and place it in maintenance's hands. Then they say, *Okay, I maybe able to fit it in tomorrow.* Those are famous last words.

You have to realize that some maintenance teams of two or three people are responsible for 500 to 1,000 units. They may get an emergency call five minutes after your simple request. Other times, they may be locked out or might have to order a part to complete a repair. In their busyness, they may forget to inform the resident or you of every move they make. They've got a tough job, and I want to acknowledge that. You have to cut them some slack.

But it's not good when a resident returns home believing a repair has been made, only to find out that it wasn't. Even worse is when there is no explanation as to why.

> *Handle maintenance properly, and half the battle is won.*

Unfortunately, miscommunication on the part of maintenance reflects poorly on YOU instead of them—even if you didn't know about a delay.

For your first couple months as resident manager, you have to keep an eye on the maintenance process. Let maintenance know you will be checking how satisfied residents are with their response time. Nine times out of 10, the maintenance staff will step up their game.

Handle maintenance properly, and half the battle is won.

9.   When setting up the initial agreement with the owner, think ahead.

Maximize your value and compensation. Think of how you can get more in trade for having more duties delegated to you. What I mean is: Focus on the "value-added" duties that cost you little time, yet may have a big impact on the property and that are highly valued by the owner. Many duties can easily be automated or outsourced.

If the owner offers half off rent, ask how you could get the full month's rent covered. They may say, "Make sure the sidewalk is shoveled and salted, and mow that little area of grass in the front." They may currently pay for services that cost them as much or more than the other half of the value of your rent. Plus, they know you are already on-site and don't have a list of 10 other clients to service first.

Let's take the sidewalk shoveling as an example and you are receiving $300 off your rent for this service. Does the sidewalk need to be shoveled after every snowfall? Perhaps you would rather pay a trustworthy neighbor $10 to $15 for the 20 minutes of work than do it yourself. Keep in mind that you are still responsible for having the walk cleaned and salted per your agreement with the owner/management company. Can you have the walk done for less than $100 a month by having someone else do it? *One seasonal duty can net you another $200 off rent every month and you didn't even do the work yourself!*

> *One seasonal duty can net you another $200 off rent every month and you didn't even do the work yourself!*

Perhaps you would like the owner to cover your Internet costs. Tell them you'll need to answer email inquiries at home and not just at your other job. You could suggest that you would keep their website up to date and take new photos for the site, or that you could set up a *simple* WordPress[11] website for them. Setting up a website and taking photos can be 90 percent work up front then 10 percent work updating over the year.

What are you good at? Offer your skills in return for a cut in rent.

You have the unique opportunity to bring a new perspective to a property that needed new management. You are presenting the owner/manager with fresh information about how things actually look and ideas about how to make things better.

10. Keep the building and grounds well maintained.

Nothing is more distressing to owner then when they drive by their property and see trash in the bushes, the roof gutter hanging from the fascia or a car up on blocks in the parking lot. Not only is it distressing, it can downright infuriate them. They have hired you to keep the place looking good, and then they see this sign of poor management from a mere drive-by. Whatever shall they see if they get out of the car and walk around the property?

---

11   Make a beautiful website for free. There are lots of free templates and help at wordpress.org.

It is like a restaurant with an unclean restroom. The manager of the restaurant *knows* patrons see the restrooms. So when one is unclean or out of paper towels, or they had to lock one of the stalls because the toilet is not working, I am always left wondering what condition things are in in the areas I can't see—like the kitchen, the food pantry and the walk-in cooler.

You can keep the owner happy by keeping the grounds and buildings looking great. Don't keep the place looking good just from the street. Going beyond creating "curb appeal" is vital to the property's success and your success as a Community Executive. Serious prospective renters don't just drive by a property—they get out and walk around. You want to maintain the exterior of the property to reflect the quality of the manager and set the tone for the quality of residents you expect to live there.

11. Maintain high occupancy.

High occupancy equals more cash flow. It is also an indicator that you are doing your job well. High occupancy is usually a direct reflection of a highly desirable property. The ideas laid out in this book are designed to get you to the highest occupancy rate possible for your property.

When you improve the occupancy rate, you will want to let the owner know of your positive progress. Don't be overly enthusiastic about it, like you just caught a big fish, shouting, "I got one! I got one!" Remember, this is your job—you are a professional, right? After you get a couple units rented, calmly and confidently let the owner or management company know about your recent progress. Also, note that tracking where your leads came from will help you target your audience for the next advertising campaign or promotion.

12. Be available for the owner to contact you whenever they would like.

Contrary to what you may be thinking, you do not have to sit by the phone 24 hours a day, seven days a week, waiting for the owner to call. "Contact" merely entails being reachable. If they call you and leave a message, you call them back immediately—even if you believe the conversation may be a negative comment on how things look at the property or about an issue with a problem resident. They are your boss—if you aren't reachable by phone, they will more than likely knock on your door to talk to you. Don't make them come down to your apartment!

What this means for us is that the owner normally leaves a message for me to call him back—period. When I hear that, I pick up the phone and call him right then and there. I don't wait until our time set aside to return phone calls. I don't want to get a second message from him. The calls usually have to do with me meeting him to point out that one problem with the roof or where I was thinking that the new landscaping boulders should go. It doesn't matter if the call doesn't seem frantic—you need to be there for the owner.

Imagine for a moment you are the owner. You are on vacation in California for two weeks with your family. When waiting for your lunch to arrive at a fine restaurant, you overhear on CNN that a tornado came through the town where your apartment complex is and has leveled dozens of buildings in the area. You also hear that the storm caused an estimated $20 million of hail damage.

You call your resident manager once, and there is no response. You pull out your cell phone and set it in front of you—constantly checking to see if you have service and that you haven't gotten any voicemails. You begin to wonder if the cell towers are down.

Twelve hours later, you call again—and again, no one responds. You may now be thinking that there is a problem with your property—perhaps the buildings have been leveled, and there are residents who are injured or even worse. Whom do you contact next to survey the damage? If you don't have a management office staff and you rely completely on your resident manager to run things, you may have to start making plans to fly back. This is not a mental exercise that you want the owner of your property to go through.

Give the owner your cell phone number and let him know he can call you at that number any time of day or night. By saying that, he will feel more assurance that you are there for him. More than likely, he will respect your privacy, family time, full-time job hours and so forth. What is important is merely the gesture, which conveys to him that he, unlike anyone else, is special and has complete access to you.

In the six years we have been at our current property, we have received a total of about 10 calls from the owner. Once was to have us assist an insurance adjuster who was stopping by to check the buildings for hail damage. He had heard that a violent storm had gone through our area and wanted to make sure everything was okay.

The idea here is be available to the owner. More times than not, they will not pester you with phone calls.

A Word of Warning

Never, ever do anything questionably unethical. This is a great rule to live by as a manager and for life in general. I want you to know right here and now that violating this rule WILL come back to bite you! Not "might"—WILL!

A close friend of ours was asked by the head manager of a property management company to falsify documents. The property had a couple of loud, obnoxious and destructive residents whom the company wanted to evict. The manager had an associate write up the eviction without giving the residents the sufficient number of warnings as stated in their lease agreement. The residents quickly retaliated with a request from their attorney to show that any notices to "remedy or vacate" had ever been delivered. Our friend was asked to support the head manager's position by creating and backdating two such notices. Of course, there was the possibility that the forgery would never have been found out; but it is not the prospect of getting caught that should deter you from doing such a thing—you should want to be abide the law and do what is right. Fortunately, our friend refused to comply with her superior.

Falsifying documents is highly illegal and highly unethical. Never, ever backdate or falsify information about yourself or any resident. Knowingly doing so could not only get you fired, but could also land you in jail!

How You Can Lose Your Position!

Once you're in, you're in. If you do a good job—and in some cases, a mediocre one—the owner will not have any reason to let you go or replace you. There are, however, a handful of scenarios in which you could lose your position. The following are what we consider the most common of these.

Scenario #1: You're fired—you slacker!

The most likely scenario that could lead you to lose your position is completely within your control. Let's say the owner/management company lets you go because *you just didn't do your job sufficiently*. You slacked off, weren't available to talk to, didn't keep the grounds clean, didn't keep up on maintenance calls, etc. In plain English: If you do your job, you'll have a job.

Keep the buildings and grounds looking good. When the owner drives by, he will notice the great work you are doing. Keep the residents happy and the vacancy super-low, and there is absolutely no reason for them to ever let you go. They don't want to have to go through the trouble of placing the ad, interviewing and training someone they don't know for your position ever again—unless you give them good reason to.

We've actually had the pleasure of having two owners tell us that they hope we never leave. Wow, what an honor! That is what you want to shoot for. However, once you get an accolade like that, don't sit on your laurels.

Scenario # 2: The owner decides to sell the property you manage.

This second scenario may not be within your direct control, but like us, you can make good if it happens anyway.

Early on, the first property we managed was sold to a developer who had his own management team. There was no longer a need for us. We didn't fight it; we moved on. If you have had the *candid talk with the owner*, as discussed earlier, you will at least get a fair warning.

On the other hand, the owner may be selling the property to a friend who is in the same situation as he is. The friend may be buying an investment and may know very little about running a property—so he may need a Community Executive (you). In this case:

- Ask the owner if he believes that you do an outstanding job (use the adjective that you want him to agree to). If he agrees that you do, tell him that he needs to highly recommend you to the new owner, so that the property can remain in the great condition it's in and with the high occupancy you have maintained. If you get a "no" when it comes to staying on in the long term, ask to stay on for just another six months. If they cannot do six months, try to get them to extend your 30- or 60-day notice to 90 days. Get the owner to do his best to work for you to stay on.
- Ask what other properties he or the new owners own or manage, where you might apply your experience.
- Ask to be introduced to other multifamily property owners they know to help you get your next placement.
- Ask the owner *and* the management company (on separate occasions) to *at the very least* write you a letter of recommendation. This will give you much more credibility than only having the experience on your résumé. If they balk at first, let them know you will write something up and send it to them to either sign or edit. Let them know the value of their recommendation.

Another common reason a property gets sold is so that the buildings can be demolished and the land can be used for another purpose. In such a case:

- See if you can transfer to a different property.
- Get two letters of recommendation (one from the owner and one from the management company).
- Ask to be introduced to other multifamily property owners they know to help you get your next placement.

Scenario #3: The nephew wants in on the action.

Sometimes a relative of the owner hears about your position and how awesome it is. They are just starting out, and they want to someday manage all of Aunt Betty's properties. It is true that blood is thicker than water, and that alone may carry enough weight for an owner to hand you your hat.

Say: "Mrs. Griswold, I understand that Skippy would like to take over my position here. Do you agree I've been executing my duties flawlessly?" (Yes.) "Is he much more qualified or experienced than I am?" (No.) "Is there perhaps a better place for him to get his experience as a manager, rather than have them experiment with this investment of yours?"

Scenario #4: The owner goes condo.

We've seen this, but haven't experienced it directly. The owner decides that the return on his investment would be better if he were to chop up the property into individual condos. When this happens, many times the resident manager keeps their position during the transition period. Depending on the economy and the local real estate climate, this process may take months or even years. In some cases the property may become both rental units and owned condos, and the resident manager kept on indefinitely. If it happens to you:

- Know how your position has changed.
- See if you can transfer to a different property.
- Get two letters of recommendation (one from the owner and one from the management company).
- Ask to be introduced to other multifamily property owners they know to help you get your next placement.

In any of the above cases, you now have the ability to use the experience you have gleaned from being a resident manager. This will make you all the more marketable for your next position.

Chapter 10

CHICKEN-FREE: WHY EVERYONE ELSE DOES THIS WRONG

My first experience meeting a resident manager is a memorable one. I was fresh out of college and was looking for a place to live with my good friend Darren. We were going to split housing costs and become roommates the next year. Our rental budget was about $350 a month each. Back then, there were not a lot of apartment complexes with websites, so the best place to look was the newspaper. We also just drove around areas looking for *For Rent* signs in neighborhoods we knew were on the lower end of the cost spectrum.

One place didn't look so bad, so we pulled over and parked the car. We approached the building and rang the manager's doorbell. A middle-aged, scrawny, haggard-looking man opened the door and stood behind the screen in the darkness. His apartment reeked of cigarette smoke. His wardrobe consisted of a tattered baseball cap and jean-shorts. Even after that introduction, we asked to see the available apartment—why, I don't know. I figured I'd give the guy the benefit of the doubt. Perhaps he was just having a bad life…er, day.

We walked through a dim hallway to the lower-level apartment. The light fixtures in the ceiling were burned out or missing. As we navigated the dark tunnel, we enjoyed the medley of aromas—cooking meat, trash, smoke. My thought was: *How can we get out of here?* We saw the pathetic apartment, finished the tour and left. It was one of those places you want to take a shower after visiting.

Not only were we scared away from living there, but the experience left an impression on me to this day. This manager was the personality someone had hired to set the tone of their property and represent them. It was hard to believe, after that experience, that people would decide to rent there—but people had. I look back now and see how, every step of the way, the resident manager was in charge of the environment we experienced. He could have controlled at least 90 percent of the quality of our experience.

He could have:

- Had office hours posted on his door or not answered the door if he wasn't presentable
- Been dressed better and improved his hygiene
- Welcomed us verbally, so that we didn't feel so awkward, as if we were bothering him
- Given us a flyer or handout with a floor plan, amenities, rent prices and rent specials, or at least had them in a box outside by the doorbell. A simple black-and-white photocopy would have sufficed.
- Replaced broken and missing light bulbs
- Cleaned up the grounds and the interior common areas
- Vacuumed the hallway or had the janitor vacuum
- Aired out the common area and put air fresheners in strategic locations
- Prepared available units for show and cared for the property overall

If a person like this could be hired and keep his position and get people to rent apartments, YOU CAN DO IT TOO!

Many owners self-manage because this is what they think they will get— some lowlife who doesn't care a rip

Question: *What must you change to attract the residents you want?*

about the property, or just another freeloader looking for a handout.

Imagine experiencing that and thinking, *Now, this is where I want to live! Where do I sign?* Don't get me wrong—I'm not knocking low rent housing. It can be clean, orderly, bright and neat. The fact that some owners will justify the poor conditions of their property by citing the low rent is pure bull. It is more like mismanagement of finances, poor planning, laziness or just plain greed. There is no excuse for it.

The owner may not want to put a lot of money into a property—so residents get used appliances, and replacing drafty windows is not a priority. When you as a Community Executive allow a property to look bad, to fall into disrepair, or don't respond to maintenance requests in a timely manner, you are on a downward spiral toward failure. Because the type of residents you will attract are not the ones you want!

Fiona also manages a 53-unit apartment complex where the rent starts at $445 a month. That doesn't mean that since the rent is low, we let the place go! We keep it clean, quiet and safe, and maintenance is handled in a timely manner. The appliances aren't all new, the carpet isn't new, and the wood trim is still dark walnut in half of the units, but it *is* clean, quiet and safe. We don't allow residents to break the rules, either. The rules are enforced, and if residents don't heed warnings, they are evicted!

Don't Play Chicken—Be the Captain

Let me remind you right here and now that *YOU ARE NOT A MOTHER HEN!* Many resident managers I have talked to or interviewed in writing this book never wander far from their property. It has become their ball and chain. That isn't the owner's fault—it is theirs. This is pretty harsh for many people to hear, but the truth is that every resident manager:

- at one time agreed to the work-in-trade negotiated before the position began
- set the tone for the property
- set the hours of operation—at least to some extent
- set each resident's expectations of them
- set the means as to how and when residents could contact them
- defined what an emergency was and wasn't
- defined their relationship with residents

Set Boundaries

What I have found is that several resident managers have *the need to feel needed.* Others have never taken the time to set up a system that streamlines things. Fiona and I set up a system strictly out of necessity. We started with full-time jobs and/or businesses to run, and later had a child, and then another baby in the midst of all of it. We needed to manage our time well to prevent insanity. Plus, we wanted to travel—and as you know, hens don't fly very far from the henhouse.

Many times resident managers find themselves working at all hours—a little here and a little there. Their time is nickeled-and-dimed away. A five-minute interruption to pick up trash here and a 10-minute interruption on a phone call there throughout the day, every day, turns resident managing into a costly and frustrating endeavor. A conversation with a lonely resident can last a half hour or more. We don't have an open-door policy and don't think you should either. Keep your home private. Set up the boundaries before they are breached, and then stick to them.

> *Grace has its place, but if continually abused, it is no longer grace—it is mismanagement.*

Residents Respond to Rules

Rules, unfortunately, are only for those who break them. When they are broken, respond swiftly by confronting residents about the incident. In almost every case, they will admit to the folly. Let your lease do the talking.

They read, agreed to and signed it all. The onus is on them to cooperate and live up to their side of the agreement.

Don't be the mother hen of the henhouse, sitting on your nest, patiently waiting for the sound of a cracking shell and then springing into action. If you are, your chick will hatch, and then it will be your job to find food, protect and coddle it, and never wander far. But you are not the residents' servant. You are there to make sure things run smoothly.

YOU ARE THE CAPTAIN OF THIS SHIP. You are in control and able to go where you want with an adjustment to the rudder. You harness the energy to steer the ship in a direction worth going.

If as captain you adhere to the rules of the contracts, lay down the law and keep a tight ship, you will sail for as long as you care to. Let the property descend into a downward spiral, and it's over. Let residents get away with nonpayment of rent, working on their cars in the parking lot, drinking alcohol out on the front steps or partying until 3 a.m., and you'll have a mutiny on your hands.

There is no walking the plank or corporal punishment here, but you must let every incident be an opportunity to display your authority as manager. Give them written and verbal notices and cite the lines of the lease and addendums they agreed to uphold to. If they disregard your notice, photocopy the part of the lease that states the rule along with their signature next to it. Keep copies of their notices in their file for your records.

Grace has its place, but if continually abused, it is no longer grace—it is mismanagement.

Statistics have shown that most property managers suffer from burnout within a few years. This is usually due to the absence of a proper system or defined schedule to abide by.

You don't have to overwork it and you don't have to babysit. You need to set up an efficient system and work that.

Take Charge! A Peek at Streamlining in Action

At the time of this writing, the only time Fiona and I answer the phone during the daytime is during the month of April—and only when we feel like answering. Why is that? April is the month that everyone in our area scrambles for a place to live for June thru August. I look at every one of those calls as a potential contract. Usually, we return calls at 4 p.m. Monday through Saturday. We take Sunday off completely, for family.

We had 10 openings this year—that was roughly 30 percent turnover. It was considered abnormally high for us. We found that many people were ending their leases with us and were taking advantage of extremely low home prices and additional federal incentives for purchasing a home.

In a three-week stretch, we've had 20 showings—ten of those prospective residents became renters with us. Two applied, but were too late to get in this year. Once we got down to the last three available units for the season, everyone felt the pressure to sign right away. Most of those showings were back-to-back showings.

I show apartments while Fiona watches the kids, and Fiona shows the apartments while I take the kids out for gelato or hit the library. I have showed apartments with one kid in a backpack and another by my side. This isn't ideal or the most professional, yet *my closing rates were the same*. It isn't that difficult. We work it out between the two of us. People say, *Well that's easy for you guys—there are two of you working together as Community Executives*. Well, we also do it with two very active and vocal toddlers.

We keep the property at full occupancy, at the highest rents in the neighborhood without any rent specials. We found a good property to manage. We keep the property looking nice and stay on good terms with our residents. Thankfully, we have learned how to keep rents at the top of our market and stay fully occupied year-round.

We have an average of three maintenance orders every two days. More people will call to see apartments for this fall, but our voicemail message will tell them we have no vacancies until *next year*. It will also tell them that *more information on our other locations can be found by calling* the company's main office phone number.

You don't have to overwork it, and you don't have to babysit. You need to set up an efficient system and work that. Don't expect everything to be easy your first three to four months. Take your time, study your residents' needs, study your market, and study your rental cycles—and then work it.

Chapter 11

THE FLYWHEEL EFFECT: STREAMLINING YOUR DAY-TO-DAY DUTIES

This chapter is about *the secret sauce*. By now you have figured out that this isn't a book on how to be a property manager, because there are more than enough books on property management, landlording and fee management. Most are stale, textbook-style works in need of a bit of updating and a more *relaxed tone*. The following pages, on the other hand, touch upon the core system that Fiona and I teach.

A Community Executive is savvy and efficient. They think like property owners and are more about managing people and setting up systems than they are about being glorified babysitters with a dust mop and plunger.

It turns out that the burnout rate for property managers is two to five years! Using an outdated system or no system at all will do that.

So how do you set up management in such a way that it becomes more streamlined?

These four processes will allow you to streamline your job quickly:

1. **Front-loading**
2. **Neglecting**
3. **Batching**
4. **Automating**

Front-Loading

Frontloading is where you take the most time organizing and setting up your systems. The first month will probably be your busiest, as you acclimate to your position. Getting all the information from the owner is essential to getting a solid start. Most owners/managers will give you a box of papers, old fliers, rings of unlabeled keys and manuals from appliances they purchased eight years ago. Once you take possession of the box, go through it with a fine-tooth comb.

Fair Housing and Local Ordinances

Call a local apartment association, multifamily organization, investment club or city/county department of housing to get the proper documents that define additional *local Fair Housing standards* and multifamily ordinances. Many ma-and-pa property owners will not have these documents available for you. Make it your responsibility to get them before you even move in.[12]

The Keys

When the owner or management company hands you the keys, ask what each one opens. Be sure to label each one then and there with a pen and masking tape, so that you don't have to try every key for each lock you wish to open over the next few days.

Having locks mastered is more convenient than having to fumble through a large key ring with 36 keys on it.

12 See http://www.hud.gov/offices/fheo/FHLaws/yourrights.cfm and check with your state and municipality for additional local policies, as well.

If the keys are not mastered (if there isn't one key that can open all the apartments and common areas), get a couple locksmiths to bid on the job for you. The owner or management company may or may not be thrilled by the idea. But having locks mastered is more convenient than having to fumble through a large key ring with 36 keys on it.

Key Vault

A master key can also be placed in an emergency access key vault *(sometimes called* a *Knox box)*. This box, placed on the outside of a building near the main exits, allows emergency service personnel to access any apartment or common area quickly, without having to break down doors. Check with your local fire department to see how you can have one installed. After installation, the box can only be opened with a special key that only local emergency service personnel have.

Key Lockbox

Depending on your relationship with the contractors you use, installing a *key box* or *key lockbox* may be a wise move. Over the years, we have seen a variety of key policies in use among contractors, owners and management companies. Here are a few of them:

- Master keys given to plumbers, HVAC, painters and cleaning crews to keep for term of service contract
- Doors left unlocked during an apartment's vacancy
- Keys hidden above door frames or under welcome mat
- Access to master key through combination-locked key box given to trusted contractors
- Resident manager personally meets and unlocks door for each contractor
- Contractor stops by main office to pick up key before going to work site

We personally have given lockbox access to contractors we trust and who are also bonded and insured. It is extremely beneficial for the contractor and the manager to have that trust.

Lockboxes are also great time-savers. They can save you travel and hours of time meeting contractors at your buildings at a specific time. I have personally waited for contractors to show up—hours after our scheduled appointment. I learned early on to communicate with a contractor that I will be making a special trip to meet them, and that I would appreciate a call from them *before* our scheduled appointment if they will be running late. Just because you live on-site does not mean you have the ability to sit around and wait for them.

The concern that management companies may have with key boxes is that keys may fall into the wrong hands. This can mean that all of the locks have to be remastered. This is a genuine possibility and must be considered when looking at giving master keys to anyone—whether a lockbox is involved or not. It doesn't have to be a contractor that misuses the privileges of holding a master key. We have heard of an incident in which an employee, trusted with master keys, misused his ability to access apartments and was fired because of it. After the employee was fired, *more than 100 locks had to be remastered.*

As I have stated earlier, we closely guard who has access to our keys and have developed an acceptable level of comfort sharing that access with individuals we know and trust.

Resident and Property Files

Get this paperwork from the owner/manager:

- Resident files (if applicable, sometimes this is kept at the main office or with the owner)
- List of tenants' names
- List of pets on-site
- List of contractors the owner trusts
- Lease end dates
- Resident vehicle information

Create a simple file system; smaller properties should only require a few file folders for all of your papers. Buy a portable hanging file box, and label the folders immediately.

Introductions

Make sure you have a letter of introduction from the owner/manager so that the residents understand that you are the new resident manager. Introduce yourself to all the residents by knocking on their doors and giving them a flyer containing your contact information. Add a good photo of yourself on the flyer, so that they recognize you when you are walking around the property. And let them know how you want them to contact you.

Leave a blank maintenance request sheet at each unit, too. Sometimes it turns out the last manager slacked off toward the end of their term. You may hear about garbage disposals that have not been working for weeks or similar issues. **Make sure to give all the work orders that arise from these requests to maintenance and then to follow up with residents.** This is giving your new residents the first impression that you are a conscientious manager and will do the job well.

Have the owner/manager write another letter of introduction that allows you to work with outside contractors. You don't want them to have to call each contractor you need to work with. If a contractor doesn't know you and wants some proof of who you are, you can fax over this letter of introduction.

Assess the State of the Property

Do a walk-through of the property (not inside the apartments) and list items that need to be addressed. What is broken or ready to break? Who needs to clean up their deck, balcony or backyard? What hazards do you see? What opportunities for improvement or increased income do you see? Do fire extinguishers look as if they have been checked lately? Are smoke alarms and other safety equipment fully functional?

From your list, decide which projects are a priority, starting with safety concerns. Write up your suggestions and send them to the owner or manager. They will either say no, will ask you to get bids or will tell you to go ahead with the work. **Never have work done without getting bids; better yet, get quotes**. Not doing so is like handing contractors a blank check. Don't be responsible for giving an okay to a contractor who ends up charging $400 to $1,000 more than you thought.

Once a contractor is chosen, get the projects in motion and keep tabs on their progress.

Nail Down Availability for the Next 12 Months

Make a list of which apartments are vacant and which of them will be vacant within the next 12 months, so that you know what you need to rent for the next year. Get a feel for when most units are rented out. Ask the owner or management company which months tend to see more leases signed. Find out who the owner's target demographic is and where they currently advertise.

Never have work done without getting bids; better yet, get quotes.

Walk through any empty units, so that you know what they look like. If they are ready to go, take the time to shoot several good photos. Borrow or purchase a camera with a fairly wide-angle lens and a good flash to take interior shots. Fifty to 100 photos will give you a lot to choose from. To find out what cameras are good for shooting interiors, do a Google search for *best cameras for realtors*. You will find several suggestions from real estate agents who rely on a camera to take great photos of homes inside and out.

Petty Cash and Charges

If you need to buy wasp spray, flowers to plant out front, a shop broom, trash bags or other cleaning products, it can be very helpful for you to have $100 to $150 in petty cash on hand at any given time. Having to wait for the owner to drop off supplies after his weekly trip to Wal-Mart, or waiting for maintenance to swing by and set them outside your door is not the best way to acquire necessities for the property. Letting you pick them up yourself involves a little trust—*but they did just give you the keys to everyone's apartment, didn't they?*

Fiona and I have actually set up a system that works remarkably well for us. We use our own credit card and charge supplies like flooring and fixtures to it. The best part is that we get thousands of points or miles for doing so. And we never accrue any interest charges, since the management company reimburses us almost immediately.

I would only recommend this strategy to those who are already secure in their finances. If you use it the wrong way, it could end up costing you in the long run.

A Good Website = Automation

Assess the property's current website if there is one. Make sure it is up to date.

If it is poorly done, uninformative, looks antiquated or is nonexistent, create a new one from scratch. Don't feel like you must have it up in 24 hours. Give yourself 20 hours or so over the next four weeks to create a great site. The key to front-loading—the part that leads to automating much of your work—is having a website that answers *every question*. It should be an information and communications portal.

Include anything in your website that people call you about. Direct people from your voicemail, printed and online ads and printed flyers to your website for additional information.

Here is what should be included in your website to make your life easier:

- Contact information prominently displayed
- Information repurposed from older printed material. (Input the text—do not scan in).
- Testimonials
- Availability of units (dates, not number of vacancies)
- Rent prices
- Current rent specials
- Any utilities included in rent
- Rental application as a PDF—*not* a Microsoft Word .doc. With a .doc, the applicant could change or delete parts of the application.
- Frequently asked questions

- Pet policy
- Whether you accept subsidized housing vouchers – mandatory acceptance in some cities
- Average utility costs
- Contact info for local service providers
- Schools within the district
- Mass transit routes and schedules
- Map showing location of the property
- Directions to the property
- Embedded Google Maps tool (allows for directions from any location)
- Photos of the interiors and exterior of the property
- Photos of the neighborhood and local attractions
- Short walk-through video showcasing an open unit and your property
- Simple floor plan
- Measurements or dimensions of rooms
- Square feet of the different floor plans available
- Contact form
- Maintenance request form
- Payment mailing address
- Blog sharing announcements and feedback
- Comment form

Include anything in your website that people call you about. Direct people from your voicemail, printed and online ads and printed flyers to your website for additional information. When you receive a question for the first time and you have to research the answer, post the question and answer on your *Frequently Asked Questions* page online, too. Save yourself a little extra work the next time.

WordPress gives you a very easy way to build a professional website by using free templates. It is already set up with basic search-engine optimization (SEO) tools. SEO means it is easy for people who use search engines like Google and Yahoo! to find the site you made. Go to www.wordpress.org for more information.

If you don't want to create a site yourself, go to one of these websites to find someone who can build a simple one for you:

- www.guru.com
- www.elance.com
- www.odesk.com
- www.craigslist.org

Costs can range from $50 to $250, depending on the complexity of the site.

Update Your Voicemail

Put all pertinent information on the outgoing message of the voicemail for your contact number as resident manager:

- "You have reached [*your name*], [*your title*] at [*name of the property*]."
- "Residents with maintenance emergencies, please hang up and call [*emergency maintenance phone number*]."
- "Currently we have [*list your available units*]." (Listing prices may filter out some callers.)
- "Our current rent special is [*rent special, if any*]."
- "[*Name of property*] does/does not allow [*pets/dogs/cats*]." (Define the pet policy.)
- "If you would like further information or are a resident with a non-emergency maintenance request, please leave a message and we will get back to you shortly."
- "You can find out more about our community by visiting us online at [*the property website*]."
- "Thank you for calling and I look forward to talking with you!"

If you keep getting the same questions over and over, address them on your voicemail and on the website, as well.

Write your voicemail greeting, speak slowly and smile while you are recording.

Email

Set up an email address for prospects—info@myapartmentcomplexname. com or something along those lines. Then create a one-sheet auto-responder. An auto-responder in this case is just a form email that is sent back to them immediately when they email you.

In the auto-responder, thank them for contacting you. Tell them your current availability, prices, specials, pet policy and website address. Let them know someone will be responding to them within the next 24 hours.

Custom Email Address

Chances are the property already has a domain name (i.e., www.myapartmentcomplexname.com) registered. The domain registrant (godaddy.com, fatcow.com, networksolutions.com, etc.) normally also provides email addresses associated with the account.

Do not get fancy and format it to look like a webpage (HTML formatting), because many people still can't properly view HTML within their email. You must design the email for the lowest common denominator and keep it to plain text.

Keep it brief, polite and informative. Be sure to follow through as you say you will.

To activate the auto-responder in an email service like Gmail, use the *vacation* setting and leave it on. Put your auto-responder email there. Test it from a different email account. Be sure to update it as availability and specials change.

Create a separate email address for your residents—something like nancy@myapartmentcomplexname.com. This email should not have a default auto-responder message active. You can activate an auto-responder specifically for your residents when you are out of the area.

Drop Box

Contrary to popular belief, you don't need to physically receive rent checks, maintenance orders, check-in or check-out forms, or keys and garage door openers. If you have a sturdy, LOCKABLE drop box that those items will fit into, you will not need to meet with people to receive the above-mentioned items. Put a sticker on the box that states "No Cash." If you are not in charge of accepting rent payments, also display the address where payments should be sent.

iPhones and Smartphones

Let this be your excuse to finally buy a decent smartphone. I fought the idea for years, but finally found one that I am truly excited about. Both Apple OS and Google Android phones are powerful machines that will allow you to do some amazing things.

I recently purchased the latest iPhone. I started out paying $100 a month for service, but quickly realized that I could cut my bill down to $65, because I didn't need 900 minutes of talk time or 1,500 text messages or 2GB of bandwidth every month. And my previous pay-as-you-go phone had been costing me between $45 and $55 a month anyway. Paying an extra $10 to $20 to have my business at my fingertips was well worth it.

I teach how to get the most out of your iPhone and how I use it to do most of the administrative work remotely!

Once you have collected the contact information for all of the residents, put their info into your phone along, with every imaginable contractor and service provider. Also, store all important documents on your phone and secure it with an access code.

Once you have collected the contact information for all of the residents, put their info into your phone along, with every imaginable contractor and service provider. Also, store all important documents on your phone & secure it with an access code.

What about non-administrative tasks? *I can't do something like pick up trash on the grounds with it—can I?* you say. Well, I can post an ad on craigslist and later pay the respondent for completing the work from my PayPal account, using my iPhone from a beach in Tahiti. Once you realize the power of your smartphone for running *the property and your business*, you will be truly amazed as to what you can do!

Check out www.CommExAcademy.com/remote to find out how I act as a Community Executive from remote locations with my iPhone, and what the latest apps and tools I use are. I've found some great applications, specifically for the iPhone, that have made my job even easier.

Remote Desktop

If you are planning on traveling and you will not have your smartphone with you or active phone service, you can install a service such as www.LogMeIn.com or www.GoToMyPC.com on your home or office computer before you leave. These services will allow you to access data and use the applications on your home desktop from any Internet connection in the world, as if you were sitting in front of it.

You will be able to use your graphics and word processing programs and access any files or documents you need from any device with an Internet or Wi-Fi connection. If you need to use someone else's iPad or smartphone to access your files or programs, you will only be slowed by your Internet connection speed, not the processor speed of the device you are accessing your computer from. Your home computer does all of the processing.

Be sure to pay for the package that allows you to print remotely. This will help you print any documents that you lose on your travels or need to send while away.

Education

Check with your local chamber of commerce and ask where you can find out more about local multifamily associations and any classes they offer.

They can be a valuable resource for you to call upon when you have questions about your job.

This book is a great foundation for you to begin managing small to medium properties on your own. There was no way for me to write about all the facets of resident managing in a short book. **This book was designed to be a quick-start guide for people who are interested in attaining free housing fast and for the rest of their life.** We literally had to cut more than half of the content out of this book to make it easier to digest for beginners. So if you have questions that remain unanswered after reading this book, visit our website, where you will find an abundance of helpful information.

Fiona and I teach online classes, hold workshops and coach individuals on how to become Community Executives quickly and successfully. We also train groups and teams to manage their resident management programs efficiently.

Our website allows members to ask us questions, find job postings, read articles, participate in the Community Executive forum, continue your education online, learn about our live events, discover helpful tools and software, and learn more about our Community Executive Certification programs.

Everything we teach through Community Executive Training focuses on teaching a streamlined system that uses the latest technology available to manage properties efficiently, with more freedom and less busywork.

Go to www.CommExAcademy.com for more information.

Neglecting

Once you have lived on-site for a month or two and have determined the state of the property, you will know what needs to be done on a constant basis and what can be neglected. Why neglect anything? Because *there is no reason to systematize the nonessential!*

Why hold office hours when you have one to two visitors for every eight hours you are open? Could they get the same information from you by using the phone or through your website? Could they drop that check off in your locked drop box?

This isn't a retail store. Some old-fashioned property owners believe you must keep office hours because the last three out-of-work or retired resident managers did. They just sat in their apartment chain-smoking and talking to their dog while watching *The Price Is Right*! You know what I mean—you don't have time for that in your busy life. Once you set up your system and automate what is essential, nine times out of ten, office hours are not necessary for properties of 50 units or fewer. Go from *a couple hours every few days* to *by appointment only* if necessary.

Why answer the phone at all hours of the night? Why allow a resident to talk *at you* for an hour about their hamster's vet visits or their car problems? Do your job as efficiently as possible, be friendly to residents, and have a degree of availability. I spend on average *10 minutes of my life per year* with a resident after they sign the lease. Other than exchanging pleasantries here and there, the less I hear from them, the better things are going for them and for me. Learn to neglect what is unimportant to the owner and the residents.

Batching

Manual Labor

If manual labor such as cleaning hallways or taking out the trash is part of your duties, choose a day or days to take care of it. When you don't schedule them, jobs like this take much longer. Set the boundaries of when you are on the clock and when you are not. I pick up trash around the property on Sundays while I'm taking out *my* trash. If you work as a couple or have children capable of helping out, assign tasks as you would in your own house. The fact is that maintaining most smaller rental properties takes about the same amount of time as it would to maintain your own house—*or less*. Most resident manager positions do not require you to do everything you would for your own home.

Showing and Leasing

You are now ready to start leasing the apartments that are either vacant now or that will be available within the next few months. Always check over apartments before showing them. Tidy them up a bit before each showing.

We have found that August 1 is our most in-demand date for leases to start. In February and March, we start receiving calls about fall availability. Once you know your local rental cycle, start to arrange your lease start and end dates around it. Doing so will make renting your property out much easier.

We went from having seven vacant units when we started managing our current property to maintaining a waiting list every spring.

When people start calling about seeing an apartment, we let them know that there is a waiting list. (Only say this if it is true.) Being able to truthfully say it is a HUGE bonus. Why? People instinctively want what they can't have. It adds exclusivity to your property.

Once we know what we have available, we set up showings for a Saturday. We book appointments 20 minutes apart. This year we had eight showings back-to-back for five available apartments on one Saturday. The following day we had another three. As people arrived. they saw other people leaving. They had to wait a few minutes just to see the apartment. That weekend we leased all the units and had to cancel the other showings! Why? *The perception of scarcity.* They knew they had to make a decision right then and there. As they sat in their car deliberating, they watched the next couple show up, and then a few minutes later, another group.

Two parties called us back on Monday and we had to tell them there were no more vacancies. They were disappointed since by waiting they lost the apartment. We've actually had people ask us to put them on a waiting list for the next available opening or for us to contact them the next rental season! That is high demand.

When we have previous leases end in the winter due to job changes, residents buying a home, other sublet situation or how the previous manager wrote the lease, we make the next lease for six or eight months. This allows us to get the lease terms to all come up for renewal in our high season.

End all leases at NOON on the last day of the month. Remind residents in advance that they must be out by noon. Have all leases start on or after noon on the first of the month. This gives your turnover crew 24 hours to paint, clean, do maintenance and steam the carpets.

Setting up our leasing strategy this way is important. It means less work for us and a happier owner. He loves the fact that everything is rented early in the year. It gives him a sense of security in an insecure market.

We are familiar with the argument that if the apartments rent that quickly then you are not charging enough. In our case, we are at the top end of the market. Besides, the lost rent for one vacant apartment for one month can be more costly than a $15.00 rent increase.

Hold the Phone

After you have front-loaded your systems and your units are all leased, I want you to try something bold: Stop answering the phone all the time! Stop babysitting the property like you are so important! Start by not answering calls during mealtimes. Then don't answer calls during family time. Then, not until 4 p.m. and not after 4:30 p.m. Also never answer the phone when you are in a bad mood or the kids are screaming. This will leave a poor impression to a first time caller.

If you have a 24-hour emergency maintenance person and you continually answer the phone with "I'm sorry, we don't have any units available until next year," why bother answering at all? Have your voicemail and website do the screening and pre-selling for you.

Only give VIPs like the owner, maintenance crew, property managers and important contractors your cell phone number. Once you program all of their numbers into it, you will be able to tell who is calling and if it is vital to answer.

For the last year, we have rarely answered the phone. We check messages at 4 p.m. and return phone calls then.

We found that the property ran just fine while we were busy at our full-time day jobs. We would come home and return calls right before dinner. After we left our full-time jobs, we kept the practice, since it worked. When we would call people back during the day, we ended up just playing phone tag anyway—people either couldn't answer their cell phone while at work, or we'd just ring into their empty apartment. Batch your phone usage and you will cut out a lot of the interruptions in your day.

If it is a maintenance issue, they will leave a message. If it is a maintenance emergency, they will call the emergency maintenance number. It is as simple as that.

Work Orders

Maintenance calls that come in throughout the day are recorded and forwarded to the maintenance team after we check the voicemail at four. We simply write up orders on a spiral-bound, triplicate work order book, and then call the maintenance supervisor and let him or her know that there are work orders waiting. If one is somehow urgent, we give the supervisor more details over the phone.

If your maintenance crew is more tech-savvy, you can send the orders to their mobile devices or via email, or simply let them know via text message that there are work orders to pick up.

To have more residents bypass you completely, have a maintenance request form installed on your website. If you do this, however, be sure you are copied on each request and check on the orders' statuses regularly.

Make Resident Files Portable

Have all of the residents' names, contact information and vehicle information with lease end dates on one sheet as a quick guide. Always update this if there is a change in any of the above.

If you own a smartphone, be smart and use it. Enter all pertinent information about residents in it, so you can have it with you all the time. Use the phone to photograph documents, keep track of lease end dates and for photos of any damages that you note upon a residents move-out. Use your smartphone to consolidate all of your resident information. Back it up to your local computer regularly.

Automating

Once your system is in place, it is merely a matter of working it. If you have tested it for several months, and it works without a hitch, write it up and bind it in a three-ring.

When you have a thorough website, an informative voicemail, and a drop box and info box for prospects to receive information, a good chunk of your administrative work is done.

How PROSPECTS contact a *Community Executive:*

- **Phone** = Standard voicemail
- **Internet** = Thorough website
- **Email** = info@myapartmentcomplexname.com auto-responder/ vacation setting with pertinent information emailed back to them immediately
- **Stopping by** = Info box with full-color flyer, website address, current and upcoming unit availability, application and screening policy stapled together

How RESIDENTS communicate with a *Community Executive:*

- **Phone** = Standard voicemail
- **Cell phone** = *VIP access only (I'm not joking)*
- **Internet** = Maintenance request form, payment mailing addresses, policies and service information (phone, cable and utility company contact info)

- **Email** = nancy@myapartmentcomplexname.com (different from the prospect email address with no auto-responder)
- **Stopping by** = Drop box to hand in completed forms, keys, leases, maintenance requests, etc.
- **In-person meeting** = By appointment
- **Emergency maintenance phone** = Direct to company maintenance or an outside contractor

Set up the above systems, and you will drastically reduce your workload.

What Just Happened?

The funny thing I found after I set up all our automated systems is that things became very quiet. It was a little disconcerting at first. We were at full occupancy, and turnover was months away. It was then that I accepted the fact that I didn't have to be busy all the time to be doing my job well.

The phone didn't ring as much anymore. We didn't get as many emails as we used to. Fewer people stopped by to ask questions. Those who left messages on our voicemail were residents with non-emergency maintenance requests and prospects who had checked out our website and already knew all about our property. People who drove up to knock on the door were instead picking up a flyer, looking through it and hopping back in their car.

> *The funny thing I found after I set up all our automated systems is that things became very quiet. It was a little disconcerting at first. We were at full occupancy, and turnover was months away. It was then that I accepted the fact that I didn't have to be busy all the time to be doing my job well.*

Automating pre-sells prospects and weeds out time-wasters. You don't have to personally answer the same questions every day. Prospects see what the units look like and know where they are located. They know the availability, square footage and price of units. If they call after all of that, they are serious about renting.

We soon were getting applications from people from out of state and overseas. They were renting our apartments and town houses by viewing the photos and reading the descriptions of our property on our website. This is a trend that we see growing. Every year we receive several applications from people we have never met—many times we don't meet them in person until move-in day.

Automation sets expectations for prospects and residents. There are fewer questions, because you have already answered them! Automation tells them what they need to do and where to get answers.

When you start out with high vacancy, you may want to answer the phone and screen prospects through a short conversation. However, when you have the *flywheel* humming along, why spend your time on the phone answering repetitive questions?

So what do you do to draw more prospects to your property and then convert them to leasers?

We soon were getting applications from people from out of state and overseas. They were renting our apartments and town houses by viewing the photos and reading the descriptions of our property on our website. This is a trend that we see growing. Every year we receive several applications from people we have never met—many times we don't meet them in person until move-in day.

Chapter 12

SALES & MARKETING: GETTING MORE LOOKERS AND CONVERTING THEM TO LEASERS

Now that you have a good handle on what your property is like, you are much more capable of being a knowledgeable salesperson. Most people say that they are terrible at selling or that they hate selling to people. I would have to agree that I don't like *selling* either. However, if you have a good product—like clean, well-priced apartments in a decent location with a responsive staff—it gets a lot easier to "sell" by merely pointing out these features with a friendly attitude.

So if you don't like selling, then by all means don't sell—just *educate* prospects about what you have to offer. It goes a little deeper than this, but I assure you that it isn't complicated.

But first, you need to get people to know that your property exists and get them interested enough to take the next step.

> *If you don't like selling, then by all means don't sell; just educate them on what you have to offer.*

Get More Lookers

If your property is hurting and you need to fill units, don't just sit in your apartment and place another $85 ad in the newspaper or local apartment guide.

Acquire an inexpensive three-in-one color printer, scanner and copier (they start at around $50), and print some simple ads. They don't have to be graphically spectacular. Just keep them clean and neat and state your property's features and prices.

Think creatively and get out and meet some people, if necessary. Here are a few places we've advertised to maintain near 100 percent occupancy for the last six years:

For free:

- **craigslist.org.** List the property every three to four days. Run one ad for your 2-bedroom apartment and another ad for your 3-bedroom apartment. Don't run identical ads at the same time or in different areas of town. You can get your account banned for doing it. Ads that don't look polished can sometimes sell better because they look more personal.
- **Grocery store bulletin boards.** Print up a simple, colorful ad with tear-off info strips on the bottom. Include photos, your website address and a call to action (e.g., "One Month Free"). Each tear-off strip should include your email address, website and phone number.
- **Tech school or university bulletin boards (physical).** Just like the grocery store ad, but tailor the copy more toward students by highlighting features of your property that would appeal to them.
- **Tech school or university bulletin boards (online).** Run a variation of your craigslist ad.
- **Local medium to large businesses.** Ask them to place your ad in their break room or on their bulletin board. Offer their employees discounts or offer a referral bonus to their employer for every employee who signs a lease.

- **Small neighboring businesses.** Introduce yourself to the owner or manager and give them a flyer. Let them know that you would like to extend an unadvertised rental discount to their employees. Remind the owner or manager that their employee would be living just a short walking distance from work.
- **Flyers in an info box out front.** Print up some nice color flyers. Have the owner invest $50 to have a graphic designer make up a Microsoft Word document with the old flyer text and your new pictures. Be sure you can update the document on your own, and do so when necessary.

For a fee:

- Glossy apartment guides and magazines: Every midsize to major city has them. They are the free printed apartment listings magazines found at bus stops, grocery stores and in the lobbies of small businesses. Though they are free to the end user, they can be very expensive to advertisers. If you do use the glossy guides, never pay the book rate. Ask for discounts.
- Top apartment listing websites:
  - www.apartments.com
  - www.apartmentguide.com
  - www.forrent.com
  - www.apartmentfinder.com
  - www.mynewplace.com
  - www.apartmentsearch.com

If the owner or management company of your property are currently running advertisements using guides or websites, find out how many leads are actually being generated by them. If the ads don't draw new leads, by all means change the ad or stop advertising with that publication or site.

If no paid ads are running, see if the owner will give you a budget to advertise to get the units rented. If each empty unit equates to $1,000 of lost rent every month, doesn't it make sense to spend at least $500 to $1,000 on advertising to fill the four units that are currently vacant?

Referrals:

Here is where it starts to get more creative. To know what is a good commission or referral for a lead or a signed lease, you need to put a dollar value on it. Here are just a few ideas:

- Pay residents or non-residents for every qualified lead—$5 for every lead that becomes a scheduled appointment.
- Pay residents and non-residents for every signed lease—$50 to $150 or more, depending on terms of the new lease.
- Network with neighboring apartment complexes and competitors. When you are full and your competitor is still looking for renters, refer them to your competitors. Ask that they reciprocate.
- Pay for referrals from neighboring apartment complexes and competitors if the referred client leases with you—$50 to $150 or more, depending on lease terms.

If you pay $5 per qualified lead but are not getting any people to sign leases, you either need to go back and redefine what a qualified lead is or work on your sales skills.

The goal is to pay as little as possible for advertising and have a fully occupied property and a waiting list. What are your competitors doing? What are the big players doing with referrals? If you're not sure, call and ask them what their referral program is.

Many times leasing agents (people who show apartments and help applicants fill out paperwork) know that a given rent amount is flexible. So if they are asking $1,100 a month for an apartment, they may already have authorization to bring the rent down $50 to $100 (or more) to fill the vacancy then and there.

Any referral, commission or special that you want to implement must be discussed and agreed upon by the owners or management companies since it will be their expense.

> If you can get written permission to take photos of a resident's nicely furnished apartment, do it. Nice furnishings will add character to your property and make it easier to sell online and in print than an empty-box apartment that lacks character. If you don't have a nicely furnished apartment available, go with a clean, bright empty unit.

Running Ads

Here is what should be included in every ad you run. You need to know what draws the right kind of people to your neighborhood. At first, you might start by advertising to everyone; however, you must at some point start targeting your marketing a bit.

What to include in a long advertisement:

- **Name of the community.** You should have a memorable and unique name, not just an address. Be sure that the name communicates only positive emotions. If the name is "Bates Estates," you may want to change it to one without so much cultural baggage. If the times have changed and the name of your community now carries a negative connotation, change it.

- **Photos.** The more GOOD photos, the better. Use a digital camera to take 50 to 100 photos of the property when it looks its best. Find 8 to 10 that represent the best of your community. If you are satisfied with the photos, start to use them for all of your ads. Consistency will help people start to distinguish your property from others and build your brand. If you can get written permission to take photos of a resident's nicely furnished apartment, do it. Nice furnishings will add character to your property and make it easier to sell online and in print than an empty-box apartment that lacks character. If you don't have a nicely furnished apartment available, go with a clean, bright empty unit. For more on taking photos, go to www.CommExAcademy.com/photos.

- **Location.** Be sure that people know where the property is by listing the street address.

- **All nearby major attractions.** State the proximity of schools, popular shopping areas and major employers in minutes, not miles. Be accurate with your listing. If you have to drive 90 mph to get to the mall in four minutes, say that the mall is only 15 minutes away— not four.

- **Any utilities and services included.** Let prospects know if water, trash and recycling, or soft-water service are included with rent. You don't need to list everything they have to pay for on their own. If cable TV service is available, but for an additional fee, just state that *units are cable-ready.*

- **Price of units per month.** If units are $1,000 a month, state that the rent is $1,000 a month even if you are running a special for one month's free rent. Don't pro-rate the rent (divide a year of rent at $11,000 by 12 to calculate the monthly savings over an entire year)! Simply say, "One month free rent with every year lease."

- **Rooms and size.** Number of bedrooms, number of full bathrooms, ¾-bathrooms and ½-bathrooms. Full bathrooms have a tub, toilet and sink. ¾-bathrooms have a shower, toilet and sink. ½-bathrooms have only a toilet and sink. So you could list an apartment as "3-bed, 2 ½ bath." Also list the square feet. Some people get away with measuring the length of the first floor by the width of the first floor and listing that as the total square feet of the apartment. That number can be quite misleading—what it doesn't take into account are closets, stairways, mechanicals, cabinets, etc. A better way is to take the time to go through an apartment of each type of layout once and measure each area wall to wall, diagram the shape and add up the square feet.

- **Availability.** Do you have units available now or on August 1? If you have multiple layouts or styles, let people know when you expect other varieties to come available. If you are unsure say, "1-bedrooms available August 1. Please call for availability of other floor plans."

- **Specials.** Are you running a one-month-free special or any other incentives? We've used free TVs, PlayStations, mall gift cards, gas cards, cable, Internet access and second parking spaces as incentives. Be creative and thrifty. Free Wi-Fi may cost an owner $100 a month for 20 apartments to access, but be valued by each resident at $25 a month. That's good value to a prospective resident. Sometimes *cost to the owner* and *value to the resident* can vary tremendously. Hopefully, you have chosen a high-value, low-cost incentive and not the other way around!

- **Types of units available.** If you have efficiencies, 1-bedrooms, lofts and 2-bedrooms, make sure readers know that you have multiple offerings. Even though you may only have 1-bedrooms open, prospects who need something else might like your location and prices and check back later in the year. Many times ads in print and online linger, and you may have new readers see your ad a month or more after the ad was printed or posted. We've seen listings active over a year later.

- **Contact.** Phone number and email address. Always, always, always give the area code. See if you can get info@myapartmentcomplexname. com for an email address—it makes you look 100 times more professional than my78firebird@hotmail.com. *If you like your Hotmail account, have email forwarding set up, so that you don't have to log into two different email accounts to check your mail. You can find someone to set up simple email forwarding for you for $15-$20 dollars using craigslist.org.*

- **Tracking Advertisements.** This can be fun. If you are testing and tracking which advertisements are working best for you, you can simply ask "Where did you hear about us?" Or use a different name for each advertisement. For instance, on craigslist I could say, "Please ask for Marty at…" and in the newspaper I could say, "Please contact Fiore at…" or on Apartment Showcase it could be, "Talk to Peter at…" Any of these variations will tell you right away where the person saw the advertisement. Also, each variation is close enough to Fiona's or my first or last name to merely be considered a misprint. You can say, "Sorry—actually it's Fiona. How may I help you?"

- **Website.** Have your web address somewhere in every ad—simply www.myapartmentcomplexname.com. Keep the site up to date—if it isn't, or it doesn't function, let the owner or manager know it needs to be fixed right away. If you can't do it yourself, post your need on craigslist or guru.com and have a professional handle it. Most simple fixes are $50 or less, and new WordPress sites can cost under $250. It is vital that your website is fully functional all the time. Make www. myapartmentcomplexname.com your personal homepage, or at least bookmark it so you see it frequently.

- **Pet policy.** Let them know your pet policy up front—otherwise, you may waste your time with people who own pets that don't fit your criteria. Once you set your rules, don't bend them. If the rules say no dogs 25 pounds or over and you've been trying to rent a unit for three months, don't rent it to an applicant with a 55-pound dog.

- **Call to action.** Examples include *Call today!* or *Schedule your appointment by calling…* or *Go to* www.myapartmentcomplexname. com *for a video tour!* The call to action is an action word followed by what YOU want prospects to do. A strong call to action will make people pick up the phone or go to your website as you tell them to.

The short version of the advertisement: The short version should include all of the above ideas in one-word or one-line form. There is really nothing above that should be cut. For brevity's sake you may combine several items into flowing sentences. Paid advertising is expensive, so the more you can communicate with fewer words, the better it will be for the bottom line.

Track the Ads and Then Edit Them

A simple and effective way of tracking ads is to use the "Please ask for Marty" method mentioned earlier. Each ad can have a different *Ask for so-and-so* that lets you know where the lead came from.

Another simple technique is to list slightly different email addresses in each ad—offer22@myapartmentcomplexname.com in one, offer23@ myapartmentcomplexname.com in another—and then have them both forward to your address for prospects, or to use the phone number plus a simple two-digit extension or reference number. Or you can simply ask, "Where did you hear about us?" There are much more sophisticated ways of tracking *online* ad leads, too.

If you have placed ads in a glossy magazine or newspaper and you are not receiving calls, stop the presses! It is time to check the ad, edit it and reevaluate it. If the venue/periodical is the problem, pull the ad. If the copy is bad, find a local direct-response copywriter on craigslist and get them to take the information you have and rewrite it in a more attractive style.

If you don't want to hire a writer, an easy way to go about editing the copy is to go through a glossy apartment magazine and circle or tear out the ads that are the most visually appealing to you. Determine what it was that attracted you to them. Next, figure out which words and phrases are used in the large full-page ads. They have paid thousands of dollars for that placement; they are not going to use that prime ad space to test copy. In most cases, they either have had a professional copywriter write the ad, or it is an ad that has proven itself effective previously. Use their copy, research layout, ideas and testing to your advantage, and leapfrog from there. Leapfrogging is starting at the point that your competition has spent years and thousands of dollars to arrive at.

Person-to-Person Contact

Once a prospect learns about your apartment and is showing at least a degree of interest, they will either email or call you to get more information or schedule a showing. If you have done your job with your website, email auto-responder and voicemail, the people who call you will be VERY INTERESTED in seeing your property. They are merely confirming that what they saw on your website is what they are actually signing a lease for.

However, some time-wasters will still call you. Here are a few quick tips on pre-screening your prospects. You want to make sure they qualify before you take the time out of your day to schedule them to tour an apartment.

Usually the order in which someone lists their desires is how they prioritize their wants and needs in their mind.

First, be crystal-clear about what it is that they are looking for. If they are looking for a 2-bedroom, 2-bath, second-floor apartment that faces the lake for June 1, then it's fantastic if you have a match. If you don't, tell them what you do have or ask if they are flexible. Usually the order in which someone lists their desires is how they prioritize their wants and needs in their mind. So if you have a 1-bedroom, 1-bath on the second floor facing the lake for June 1, chances are it will not suit their list of needs.

Second, be sure they meet your qualifications. If you have a no-pets policy, ask if they have a pet. I have shown a dozen apartments only to have the person sheepishly ask me if we accept pets at the end of our tour. What a waste of time. If you have special screening criteria—e.g., strict pet policy, 55 and older community or other criteria not protected by Fair Housing—let them know up front. Whatever you say, be sure to say it to everyone who asks about visiting your property. Never judge people over the phone by their accent, vocal qualities or any apparent disability. To do so is a serious violation of Fair Housing standards. Treat everyone equally.

5 Questions to Ask When People Call

1. My name is Michelle, what is your name?
2. Where did you hear about us?
3. Do you have any pets? (you can stop here if they do and you don't accept pets)
4. What size apartment do you need?
5. When are you moving?

Converting Them to Leasers

Site Tours

Once you have pre-screened prospects, the next step is to have them visit your property. With a little preparation, you will become a pro at leasing apartments.

The exterior of your property, the location, or the description in the ad or on the new website caught their attention; it is now your responsibility to understand what attracted them and to expand upon it. Knowing what drew them to your property and what, specifically, they are looking for will tell you what to focus on.

Many times if another property on their list is comparable to yours, it comes down to *which of you is the better salesperson*. We believe that the

Many times if another property on their list is comparable to yours, it comes down to which of you is the better salesperson. We believe that the best salesperson is the one who has a great product they believe in and merely educates people on what they have to offer.

best salesperson is the one who has a great product they believe in and merely educates people about what they have to offer.

What does your property offer to people? YOU have to be sold on the property before you can sell anyone else on it. If you don't believe in your product, you will send out that "vibe."

If there are things that you don't particularly like, see what you can do about changing them. If you can't change something like traffic noise, then what *could* you like about that challenge? Perhaps you are uniquely positioned close to a bus or commuter rail that efficiently takes residents to downtown, schools and major attractions in less than five minutes.

You should point out things that you personally love or have heard other residents say they love about the property, as well.

Consider This:

You are not selling someone on renting a $1,000 apartment; you're selling someone a $12,000 apartment. The lease the prospect signs is a legally binding contract. In most cases, this obligates them to continue pay the agreed-upon amount every month for the remainder of the lease—in this example, 12 months. You are selling an item that costs more than most people at that level of income will spend on an automobile—year after year.

Preparation

Staple a flyer together with your application, screening criteria, business card testimonials and any move-in specials with an expiration date. Place a post-it note on the top right with the appointment time, their name, phone number, when they want to move in and the apartment number (s) you are showing. This is extremely helpful when you have back to back appointments. That way when they arrive, you can quickly glance at the post-it note, remove it and greet them by name.

Greeting

Greet the visitor warmly, and then hand them a flyer with all of the pertinent information about the property, specials, and so on. After you give them the flyer, point out the different areas the flyer covers, such as responsive maintenance or 24/7 emergency maintenance. **The number one reason unsatisfied residents terminate a lease is due to unresponsive maintenance.** Let them know up front how important timely maintenance is to you and the owner.

Next, give them a second sheet full of colorful testimonials from previous and current residents. Be creative with the layout of the testimonials—don't just do a series of one-liners on plain white paper.

As stated earlier, batch appointments when possible. If you know it takes you 20 minutes to show an apartment, try to get the next appointment to show up 25 minutes after the first appointment arrives. When the first visitor sees another prospect arrive to look at that same apartment, it plants the seed of scarcity in their mind. They are thinking, "This other guy might take my apartment. I've got to fill out the application ASAP!" The second prospect is thinking the same thing.

Showing the Apartment

Give 24 hours' or more notice to show any occupied unit. Know what you are getting into. Don't show a unit without having looked at it a few minutes prior. Turn on lights and open blinds to brighten up the place before entering with a prospect. If it occupied and the resident is home, be sure to ask permission to do this.

Sometimes when you post a notice to show an apartment, one resident may see your notice, but forget to share it with their roommates. You may end up surprising residents who are not expecting you to be in their apartment. You may even surprise them after shouting "Hello, office!" as you walk through the unit. This is just one more reason to walk through the unit *before* taking prospects through.

Is showing this unit going to put the community in a positive or negative light? Some explicit material or otherwise offensive material in a resident's home can turn visitors off to your entire property. Don't show a bad unit and then make a dozen excuses or put down a resident because of cleanliness or other issues. In some cases, it may be worth showing *your* apartment if the style is the same or similar. If you know you will be showing your unit on occasion, don't smoke in it. The smoke alone will lose you sales and cost you more time and money trying to lease the upcoming vacancies.

Another tip is to pay a small fee to a resident every time you show their beautiful, tidy, well-furnished apartment on short (five minutes to one hour) notice. Praise them for how they keep their home and ask if they would be willing to have $10 taken off of their rent every time you need to show their unit on short notice.

When we have done this, the owner paid the resident through a rent credit; it was not money out of our pocket. We've never had anyone turn us down yet! If this improves your closing rate 50 percent or more over showing an apartment that is an embarrassment, it is money well spent. Showing a clean unit sets a standard for prospects and attracts a higher-quality resident.

After you have done your pre-walk-through routine and know you have a tidy, unoccupied apartment to show, allow the visitor to be the first to enter a room. The rooms will look smaller with you standing in them; stand outside or off to one side.

Invite the visitor to explore a little. Don't hover, and don't give them a guided tour. Point out the main features and get out of the way. When they are finished, tell them what will be done to freshen the unit after the current resident moves out.

Ask them what they liked the most about it. Wait for their response. This will give you clues as to what to highlight in the remainder of your time together.

As you are walking them out, list amenities that are outside the unit, as well as neighborhood highlights. Ask what other questions they have. Hand them an application and let them know how and when to get it back to you.

Let them know if there is an application fee. We've set ours at $100. If the applicant bails after the background check has been completed, the management company keeps the $100 for their application processing costs. If the applicant is approved, the $100 goes toward their security deposit. If the applicant is denied, we return their $100. The purpose of the fee is to make sure applicants are serious.

For a simple closing, remind them they have your business card and point out the phone number where they can reach you. Make sure the testimonials page are right below the flyer and point this page out. These testimonials will remind them that so many people love living at your property.

***Tell them* what to do next.** Show them how easy it is to apply by completing the short application. Point out the different areas of the form. Direct them to where they may place it in your drop box later. At this point you should know how interested a prospect is in the available apartment. Your goal is to serve people. Don't try to talk them into something that isn't right for them.

When marketing your apartments, condos, flats or town houses—be yourself. You may not like selling; that's okay, because no one likes to be sold. Don't put on your salesperson hat and change your voice. There is no reason to be nervous. Just be

> *You may not like selling; that's okay, because no one likes to be sold.*

friendly, show them a good product, and answer their questions, and you will be a great at leasing.

What About Renewals?

I want to take a moment to touch upon renewals here. It costs the owner a lot of money every time a resident leaves, so keeping residents happy is cheaper for the owner in the long run. Maintaining open communication and showing that you value your residents by handling maintenance in a timely fashion and upholding a peaceful community clears up the most common reasons for residents to leave.

If you are doing the above and residents still tend to move on after a year, you can make a renewal more appealing by give good residents incentives to stay. These can be simple things like:

- New bathroom vanity
- Ceiling fan or new light fixture
- Programmable thermostat
- Touch-up painting
- Cleaning carpets
- $50 to $100 gift card
- Keeping their rent at their current rate

These incentives are relatively small costs compared with a full-blown turnover. Turning over one of our town houses can cost from $1,000 to $3,500, depending on the amount of wear and tear or damage to the apartment. Why so much? Well, the minimum apartment turnover require professional carpet cleaning ($250), paint throughout ($700), maintenance ($100) and a thorough cleaning ($150). That's the minimum! Now imagine having to change the carpet ($2,500), repairing any drywall holes ($40 per patch or more) or replacing an appliance ($350 on up!).

Since you have been providing excellent service and now are offering an update to their apartment or another small gift, why should they move?

Another added benefit of offering an update to their apartment is that it stays with the property and improves the value of the property, while strengthening the relationship with the resident. It is a win-win-win situation for you, the owner and the resident. And once your property becomes highly desirable, you may not need to offer a renewal incentive.

Chapter 13

THE MOST IMPORTANT ELEMENT: GOOD MAINTENANCE ATTRACTS AND RETAINS RESIDENTS

Most people who complain about living in a residential community tend to complain about a lot of other things in life. Many times, complainers don't go to the top first—they just talk amongst themselves about how bad their living conditions are. And it may be because one time, the maintenance man didn't follow through on something; or maybe the problem was addressed, but not well enough.

A friend of mine who writes about the growth of social media recently told me, "When people are satisfied, they tell three people; when they are dissatisfied, they tell 3,000." What on earth does that mean? It means people don't share good news like they do bad news. With the advent of Twitter, Facebook, MySpace and apartment review sites, it now only takes one tweet, post or a comment to give hundreds if not thousands of visitors a bad impression of you or your community.

Good Maintenance Is The Most Important Element

According to a survey conducted by Clearwater Research, Inc., **"Good maintenance is the most important element in attracting and retaining apartment residents."** Those who took the survey ranked appearance, condition and upkeep more important than cost of rent, security and amenities and location. Reliability of appearances was the highest rated factor when considering renewal of their lease.

Another study indicated that **80 percent of residents feel reliability of maintenance is more important when considering lease renewal.** However only 69 percent felt that their owner or management company actually delivered.

"How do Your Properties and Procedures Compare to These Surveys?" <u>Wisconsin Apartment News</u> June 2001:8

So how in the world do you stop this from happening? One word: responsiveness. People want to know that they are important to you and that they are valued customers. In many cases they are paying "you" 30 to 40 percent of their income— more than they pay anyone else in their life. The best way to show that you care is by giving them fast, reliable and high-quality service. Learn how to do this, and you will cut any losses you may have.

Just the other day I was at a close friend's apartment. She had a dishwasher that neither cleaned well nor dried the dishes. In addition, her freezer wouldn't get cold enough to keep ice cream frozen. It had been that way for five months!

I have seen this time and time again with residents. They tell me that they didn't mind that the fan was not working because they didn't want to trouble me. PLEASE! It's no trouble to me and no cost to them. It is our job to fix the stuff, but it is still residents' job to report it. Fiona and I don't raid apartments and test everything to make sure it is working properly when they are out shopping.

As for my friend, she didn't want the owner to see how she decorated the apartment by painting and putting up a new light fixture in the bedroom without asking permission. So she is willing to live with problems for the rest of her time there—at which time, she will move out and have to repaint and remove the light fixture anyway. The appliances will still be broken and will have to be fixed then. She may lose a significant part of her security deposit due to damage or negligence on her part.

Here is a scenario I have seen several times:

1. A resident's stovetop burner stops working.
2. The resident doesn't pick up the phone and call maintenance, but just uses the other burners.
3. Another burner goes out.
4. The resident talks to a neighbor about how things are falling apart.
5. The resident talks to a relative about how bad conditions are where she lives.
6. In passing, the resident mentions her stove to the resident manager when she sees her.
7. The resident manager forgets to contact maintenance about the stove because she was leaving to do grocery shopping for the day.
8. The stove goes unfixed for two months.
9. Renewal comes up.
10. The resident decides not to renew because the management doesn't care.

It seems as though it comes down to maintenance. Effective maintenance can make or break your property's viability. Some people will say that a neighbor is too loud or that they can't find parking or that rent is lower elsewhere; however, most people leave apartments due to the conditions within their own unit.

If you can get residents to tell you when they have a maintenance problem as soon as the problem occurs, you will have the opportunity to keep their unit in tip-top shape. It will keep them happier. They will know that you and the maintenance team will always respond with a timely fix.

Processing Maintenance Work Orders

Rarely do we pick up the phone when someone calls. You may say, "Isn't that being unresponsive?" Well, yes and no. We are choosing to not answer the phone at all hours of the day and night. If we know there is an ongoing issue with a resident, we may pick up.

If it is an emergency, they will hear the phone number for emergency maintenance and call them. If it is a small maintenance item, we will find out at 4 p.m. when we check our voicemail or the following morning. Once we have the maintenance request, we call it in to maintenance and then hang the work order on our drop box for them to pick up. You can have responsive service while still maintaining boundaries.

Buying a spiral-bound maintenance work-order-form book with triplicates allows you to place a detached work order in the maintenance inbox or other message area and keep a copy for yourself. This is a great way to record maintenance issues and follow up with residents at a later date. You could make your own, but for a notebook that costs a few dollars, you will have a much better system in place, and the owner or management company will pay for it.

Once you call in your request, get back to the resident. Always be sure to check that you or the maintenance team have permission to enter if they are not home. A "yes" from the resident allows your team to go in and get the job done without a lot of scheduling hassles. If the resident has a pet, be sure to note it. A cat or dog getting out of the apartment will cause more trouble for maintenance and you than you want.

Be sure to include the resident's phone number for your maintenance tech. They may have to order parts or schedule an outside contractor to handle a bigger-than-expected project. If the maintenance tech has the resident's phone number, they can contact them and let them know that they are servicing them, but that there will be a delay. There are also handy-dandy door hangers that maintenance can use to let residents know they were there, as well as to note the status of a repair.

In general, I assess maintenance problems and contact the proper contractor (e.g., plumber, electrician, heating or appliance repair person.). I give them the best detailed description of the problem I can and give them my educated guess as to what I believe is going on. I also provide them with make and model numbers of appliances or cite dimensions of pipes and holes when possible.

From there, they can prepare for the visit to our property by bringing parts and tools that may be necessary. The idea is to give them enough information that they only need to make one trip out—thus saving a second trip charge and more billable time.

So what does handling maintenance calls properly look like? First of all, you need to let your residents know before they even sign the lease how important it is to you and your maintenance team that you receive maintenance requests in a timely manner. The sooner they contact you, the sooner the issue can be addressed. You want the prospect to know that their comfort and satisfaction are Priority No. 1.

Letting prospects know up front that their maintenance requests are important to the owner, managers and maintenance team will not only build rapport with the prospect, it will also show them that you mean business. If you can get a prospect to sign a lease for a year, you now have one to two months to convince them you were telling the truth.

Communication is the key to good maintenance. Don't *over*-promise and *under*-deliver by telling your resident that maintenance will be there the same day, when they are swamped and can't get to the job until tomorrow. Be realistic.

During turnover season, maintenance can fall behind. Make sure you follow up with both maintenance and residents whenever necessary. And we've unfortunately received calls about issues we thought had been resolved by maintenance weeks prior. It doesn't have to be due to them being negligent; work orders can be misplaced, too.

Your tenants want to feel cared for. Make communication of maintenance issues a priority. Residents don't necessarily need their mini-blinds or loose doorknob fixed today; they just want to know it is being addressed and that they matter.

Chapter 14

911: WHY MOST EMERGENCIES ARE NOT *EMERGENCIES*

On August 12, 2006, Fiona and I woke up just as we did every other day. However, that day I went downstairs and saw that my mom had left me a voicemail at 6 a.m. It said, "Did you hear about the apartment fire on the Beltline?" I called her back right away. My dad answered and said, "I heard about an apartment fire on the radio, and I turned on the TV to see *my building up in flames!*"

Emergencies do happen. Fortunately, they *rarely* happen in most communities. They are the horror stories you hear about in the news and that are talked about at apartment association meetings. You don't hear about the good things that happen or the humdrum of everyday business—you hear about the tragedies.

Over 11 years of being property managers of *hundreds of units*, we've dealt with several minor and even a few major emergencies:

- Broken water pipes
- Boiler (furnace) malfunctioning in the dead of winter
- Flooded apartments
- Kitchen fires
- Arson that led to an entire multi-unit building burning down

- Break-ins
- *Faked* muggings
- Domestic abuse
- People acting crazy and breaking into a neighbor's apartment in a drug-induced state

I'm not telling you this to scare you. I just want you to understand that *emergencies do happen.* The good thing is that they rarely happen. In our almost nine years of being resident managers, we have only witnessed the first two incidents listed above at properties *where we live.*

How did we handle them?

When I saw an icicle forming on the fascia of our neighbor's garage door, I knew that their kitchen water pipes had frozen because of the subzero temperatures. When a warm spell occurred shortly after the severe cold snap, the frozen water in the pipes thawed and started leaking out. Upon recognizing this, I called our maintenance emergency number and had our responsive tech stop over and take a look at it. The process on my end took all of three minutes and a phone call.

The boiler going out was another story. We were living in the 17-room rooming house for women when the boiler pump went out. A snowstorm that had been dumping on our city since the night before was still going on.

When I called the heating company to come out and fix the boiler, they said it would be impossible for them to come out until the following morning due to road conditions. So, no heat for the night. Some of the women stayed in their rooms that night and bundled up, while others headed to friends' houses to stay. It got down to the low 50s in the house that night.

Early the following morning, Fiona and I went to a home improvement store and bought four space heaters. When we returned, we put the heaters in the common areas to keep the most people warm. The women just brought books and blankets down to the living room and chatted with each other or left to study at the library. It wasn't until later that night that the boiler was repaired.

Because we had taken the time to build a relationship with our residents, the incident was not followed by nasty letters of complaints, yelling or hard feelings. You know what? We were all in it together, and we all got through it without any scars. They had no heat; neither did we.

As Community Executive, I assess whether an incoming maintenance call is an emergency, a general maintenance issue or a more complicated affair. If it's an emergency concerning fire, the resident calls 911. In the event of a water leak, residents call emergency maintenance at any hour.

On move-in day, we give our new residents a letter defining what an emergency is and whom to contact for each type of emergency. Here is the basic list:

- Fire or crime in progress: 911 first, then our home number
- Water leak or flooding: emergency maintenance
- Gas odor: utility company first, then our home number
- Electrical issue: emergency maintenance

The way we have it set up, water leaks of any kind need to be reported to the 24-hour emergency maintenance team as soon as they are found— no matter the time. Emergency maintenance then gives the resident simple directions to temporarily stop or catch the water, or they come over and address it immediately. So what "emergencies" are we really involved with as Community Executives?

- Fire: We are involved **after** the fire department. The resident reports the fire by calling 911, and then pulls the alarm and attempts to alert neighbors. By this time, we should be getting residents safely out and acting as a liaison to the fire department.
- Crime: **after** police are contacted
- Gas odor: **after** utility company is contacted

In all of the above emergencies, the Community Executive is contacted *after* the proper emergency personnel. The emergency is already being handled; your job is to follow through.

However, not every late-night call for help is what I consider an emergency. Here are samples of "emergency" calls that we (or our emergency maintenance team) have received over the years:

What is your availability for apartments?

- *I won't be able to pay rent on the 1st. Is that okay?*
- *My car battery is dead. Can you give me a jump?*
- *The neighbor is having a party, and it's 1 a.m.*
- *My air-conditioning isn't cold enough.*
- *My garbage disposal is stuck.*
- *I have ants in my kitchen.*
- Lastly, my favorite: *My cable TV is out!*

None of the above would be considered emergencies by me or most managers.

I have had people ring the doorbell at 2 a.m. because they were locked out. Some companies outline in their non-standard rental provisions that a charge of $25 needs to be paid directly to resident managers before they can open up a unit in the case of a lock-out (after checking the resident's photo ID against rent records). Not paying rent on the 1st is a matter that can be worked out during office hours. Parties or other noise disturbances are best handled by a visit from police. Problems with a resident's car—call AAA. Cable TV is out—call your cable provider. I think you get the idea.

If you don't define exactly what is considered an actual emergency and what course of action residents should take when such situations occur, emergency calls can be an excuse for some people to selfishly bump their maintenance requests to the top of the list.

Surviving a Fire: The Whispering Oaks Apartments

Here is a real-world example of how to handle a *real emergency*. Once we understood how to deal with the worst emergency situations possible, everything else didn't seem so scary.

Fiona and I rushed over to my father's apartment building to see the damage for ourselves and to apply some order to the chaos. When we arrived, we saw about 100 residents and neighbors, firefighters and the EMS outside the charred and smoldering building. Fiona put on her leadership hat and started asking questions. The first person she went to was Becky, our point person and resident manager.

Becky had held the apartment community together by being a literal shoulder to cry on that day. When chaos set in, the residents looked to the resident manager to give them direction.

The fire chief and his crew were controlling the fire. The city had sent over a bus, for our residents to use as warm shelter. Shortly after that, the Red Cross showed up. They supported our residents with food, coffee and water. Next, Culver's restaurant sent over about 100 meals. That night and for the next two nights, the Red Cross had set up a temporary shelter for our residents who had no other place to go. They were shuttled to a nearby high school gymnasium, where food and lodging was set up for them. We visited the residents who stayed in the gym and assured them that we were going to help them in any way we could.

We also received visits that morning from other apartment managers in the neighborhood. They apprised us of their apartment availability for our residents.

I was truly amazed as to the systems that were set in place in our town to respond to disaster. When the fire was officially out, we were allowed to enter and see the building and office. Fortunately, our office was not damaged by the fire; unfortunately, it was severely damaged by smoke and the water that was used to put out the fire.

We salvaged what we could of the office. We made insurance claims for computers and furniture lost due to water, heat or smoke damage. Within 24 hours of the fire, the insurance company cut us a check, allowing Fiona and her staff to move our office to a temporary location and buy new equipment and furniture immediately.

At the time, our property management business was the biggest it had ever been. Fiona had several full- and part-time employees and hundreds of rental units all over the county. The team quickly came together and got things back to normal within 48 hours.

After the insurance's investigators searched through the debris and rubble, they centered around one area right near the front door. They determined that it was a case of arson. They interviewed everyone who worked for our company and later told us that they believed the fire had been started by someone putting a lit cigarette into the rent drop box attached to our building. There was a hole cut into the back of that style of drop box, which exposed the increasing heat to the wood siding of the building. The fire went up through the exterior wall and spread rapidly.

Lessons we've learned…

- **Have a disaster plan.** Put together an *In Case of Fire* document for residents that shows them plain directions on how to exit the building quickly. Attach it to the back of the front door of units that share hallways and stairways. Include phone numbers of whom to call. (This is mandatory in many municipalities.) It should also state that when possible, residents should close their apartment doors upon exiting. Closed doors can stop the spread of flames and smoke damage. Fire, heat and dense smoke damage spreads quickly through doors left open. Let residents know what to do in case of tornado, hurricane, earthquake, etc. (region specific). Have a map that shows them how to get out of their unit to a safe area. Attach it to the back of the front door of units that share hallways and stairways. Include phone numbers of who to call in emergency.
- **Have EVERY important phone number saved in your cell phone's contact list.**
- **Keep all current paper records in plastic boxes off the floor.**
- **Use an off-site archival storage service for paper records.**
- **Back up data to an online storage service daily.**
- **Have adequate renter's insurance for your own belongings.**

- **Highly recommend that residents purchase renter's insurance.** Renters who had rental insurance received immediate assistance and remuneration for their personal property.
- **Set up a "Bat Phone" with Google Voice.**[13] Google Voice is free and allows you to pick a unique phone number that will forward calls to multiple phones simultaneously. A call to that one number can ring your cell phone, work phone, home landline, your partner's phone, the maintenance supervisor, etc.

Emergencies do happen. If you have an emergency maintenance contact for residents to call directly, it allows you to spend more time away from the property without being tethered to the phone to answer calls at all hours. Have a plan of action that you share with your residents and your emergency maintenance team that everyone can understand, remember and follow in the case of a real emergency.

---

13 Watch a demo video at http://www.google.com/googlevoice/about.html

BENEFITS AND FREEDOMS THAT A RARE FEW ENJOY

Chapter 15

CLONE YOURSELF: PLANNING YOUR DISAPPEARING ACT

It was sweaty-hot in the room. The lights were dimmed except for a tiny glittering disco ball hanging over the kitchen sink. The noise from the '80s new wave music and the people yelling over it rang in my ears. Fiona and I were *partying like it was 1999!*

Many of us had made the strenuous hike up 6,000 feet to Refugio Otto Meiling[14] earlier that day. Fiona and I were celebrating with our new friends Marcello and Alicia, as well as about 50 other travelers—all weary from the eight-hour hike and altitude. A famous chef from Buenos Aires had made the ascent with some raw ingredients and cooking supplies earlier that day via pack mule. He had been cooking *asado* over an open fire for hours and was now preparing the side dishes for dinner.

Otto was a German immigrant and mountaineer. He had built this *refugio* (refuge) on a spit of land between two moving glaciers near the summit of the mountain. For years, travelers have used it as a base camp for their ultimate ascent to the peak of Mount Tronador—"the Thunderer."[15] The mountain was aptly named after the *thunderous* roar that can be heard for miles every

---

14 http://en.wikipedia.org/wiki/Otto_Meiling
15 http://en.wikipedia.org/wiki/Tronador

time a piece of one of the glaciers breaks off and crashes to the bottom of the valley below. It was truly a magnificent experience.

In 1999, Fiona and I wanted to take a trip we would never forget, to have an extraordinary experience that we would tell our children about. While the world anticipated the collapse of western civilization at 12 a.m. on January 1, 2000, we would be another world away, on a mountaintop where there was no electricity—save for what was supplied by a simple solar collector mounted on the outhouse.

We had made plans to have fun that New Year's and let everyone else in the world worry about their computers not turning on, the loss of years of data or companies collapsing because of corrupted files.

At that time I was working for the University of Wisconsin. Fortunately, my job allowed almost five weeks of paid vacation every single year from day one of employment (it's crazy, I know). I asked Tom, my supervisor, if it would be okay for me to take about a month off to go to Argentina. He was shocked at first—initially thinking that I would be gone for good, like the guy I had replaced.[16] But we both knew that this was the slowest time of the year. I had already trained the faculty, and school would be out for much of the time I would be away. I promised that I would return and that I would forward my phone to my two other workmates. We got **Yes #1.**

Tom gave me the green light, so I knew I was in the clear. Now it was time for Fiona. She asked (or more like *told*) her supervisor that she would be gone for those five weeks. Since they knew that I was already going, they conceded and allowed her to go, as long as everything on her end was tidied up as much as possible. **Yes #2.**

About four weeks before leaving, Fiona and I knew we had to have someone we both trusted to watch over the 17-room house we managed while we were in South America. Fortunately, we had two good friends, Nick and Lorinda, who seemed as though they could fit the part we played easily enough.

---

16 The guy before me was at his job for a month and then went to Alaska for a vacation—never to return.

Nick is a gearhead. He is the kind of guy who could take apart a Lamborghini and piece it back together in an afternoon, and make a few modifications that would improve its performance. Lorinda is a people person, one of the kindest people I have ever met. She would give a shivering stranger her coat without thinking twice, knowing that she could get another coat for herself somewhere else later.

When we asked Nick and Lorinda to watch the place for us, we didn't want to give them a huge list of all the little nitpicky things that we did on occasion—things like unclogging the industrial *Insinkerator*, testing all of the fire alarms monthly, checking the pantry for mice, emptying the coins from the laundry machines, removing unauthorized bikes from our bike rack, oiling the pump on the boiler, and so on. We merely gave them the must-do short list:

- Check the house answering machine and write down messages. Reply to the most important ones.
- Make sure the sidewalk and steps are clear of snow and are salted.
- Give residents your pager number as their maintenance and emergency contact.
- Walk through the common areas once a week.

The long list would have been intimidating, and many of the things on it would have just been tedious and unnecessary to list anyway. We chose to keep things simple. Fiona and I just did a lot of those little things right before we left to make it easier for our temporary caretakers.

That was all. For that, we paid Nick and Lorinda $100 a week. Nick would stop by the house after work every couple of days or after a snowfall to clear the sidewalk. Lorinda would check messages and return calls from home. **Yes #3.**

Last came talking to Vince and Mary—the owners of the house. We now had three *yeses*.

We had only been in place in our jobs and as resident managers for about five months, and we were asking for a five-week vacation! I understand it really was a lot to ask. Looking back, I realize now that we must have been a little crazy back then.

Vince and Mary didn't say no—but they weren't exactly excited about us leaving. But after they met Nick and Lorinda and exchanged contact information, they were satisfied with the arrangement. Finally! **Yes #4!**

To read our conversation with the owners of the property, go to
www.CommExAcademy.com/vacation

Extremely Important!

Never leave your post for more than a weekend or a couple of days without clearing it with the property management office or the owner of the property. It is rude, irresponsible and may be a breach of your contract. Imagine if they called you to check the exterior lights of the building and you told them you were in Las Vegas betting on horses for the next week, or in the Bahamas getting a tan and sipping mojitos. Or even worse, if you told them, "Sure, I'll do that!" when you were actually out of town.

Don't lie and don't give them the false sense that you are in town or on the property when you are not. The next thing they say might be, "I'll be stopping by tomorrow. Let's have lunch." (This will not end well.)

Upon finding you away from your post, the owner may wonder if you can be trusted anymore. Where are you? When are you actually around? SO DON'T DO IT! YOU MAY JUST LOSE YOUR POSITION!

They are depending on you to be there to serve the community. Your first obligation is to the owner and then to the community you are supposed to be managing. Be there for them. If you are going to go to Swaziland, don't say South Dakota. Be real and they will respect you for it. They know you need a break every now and then. If you have done your job, and the units are filled up, they will more than likely wish you well and send you on your way with their blessings. There will be no need to cover your tracks later.

It is important to think through the objections that each individual will have before approaching the owners or property manager about an extended absence. You must sell them on the idea that things will remain unchanged and duties will be taken care of while you are gone. It should be to them as if you weren't even gone.

Ask yourself these questions regarding the owner or property manager you must receive permission from:

1. Why did they really hire me? To be their eyes and ears? To be there in emergencies? For their piece of mind? To be a glorified janitor?
2. What duties have I been hired to do on a regular basis?
3. How often do I need to address each duty?
4. Can some of the tasks be done before I leave, once or twice while I am gone and then again when I return?
5. Am I willing or even able to work remotely or check in a couple times a week?
6. What is the difference between me being gone for one night, a weekend, a week, a month or three months?
7. Have they given me permission to leave for a week before? What are the main differences between being away a week versus a month?
8. Is it the distance or the duration they will be most uncomfortable with?
9. What six people would I most trust to do my duties? Couples may be better.[17]
10. Can I show them a quantifiable improvement that I have made in the last month or week before asking them? (For example, units are rented for the next five months, units are full for next season, we just received three renewal notices, the property grounds and common areas are spotless, and the new website is online.)

Answering the questions above before approaching the owner or property manager will help you think through your strategy as to how you will answer their objections.

---

17 Couples can be better to watch the property while you are away. They can split the duties according to their strengths, and can also be more available to be at the property if necessary.

**Learn another powerful strategy that can allow
you to take extended vacations at
www.CommExAcademy.com/getawaystrategy**

When we returned home from our five weeks in Argentina, the first resident we saw exclaimed, "We had the fire department here yesterday!" Apparently, a smoky smell had been coming from a light switch in the living room. They immediately called 911, and the fire department arrived.

The fire chief discovered the problem was that someone had plugged a 1,500-watt space heater into an electrical socket that was controlled by a light switch. Not good, but not a disaster either. They told our residents to not do it anymore. That was it.

The girls knew to call 911 when they smelled smoke. The 130-year-old house didn't burn down, and no one was injured. The longer you manage properties, the more you realize that most emergencies are either not really emergencies or are handled by professionals (firefighters, police, plumbers, electricians, etc.) after a simple phone call.

I begrudgingly returned to the office the next day. I turned on my computer and waited for my Windows desktop to appear. I held my breath and opened Outlook. What I saw amazed me. I had a total of two emails. I sat there shocked. First, I realized that my pre-departure emails had got out to all of the right people, so they knew to contact my workmates. Second, it reminded me that I wasn't as important as I'd thought I was.

The two emails were from faculty. One was a request for training upon my return, and the other was a frantic plea for help with a presentation that had taken place about two weeks prior. I'm sure the professor either figured it out or didn't and the world kept spinning.

You will find that once you disappear for a while, if you've put the right people in your place, given the proper notice to key people, and set up an automated system to hum along, few people will even realize you have vanished.

Chapter 16

RESET AND REDESIGN: RETURN TO YOUR FIRST LOVE AND GET PAID TO DREAM

Reset Your Thinking

The day I left my university job, I already had a secondary income stream from my multimedia business. It wasn't much, but the amount of work coming in indicated that it could be worth pursuing. So I left my university job even though friends and family told me I was "set for life" and that I was foolish for doing so. The truth was, I wasn't being challenged, nor was I happy doing the work because I knew I had been made for something different. Perhaps you can identify with what I was feeling.

I needed to make a complete change by RESETTING my way of thinking.

I recognized the potential that was there if I could recapture my finite resources of time and money and redirect them to where I saw the most "life value." For me, that meant finally following my dreams and my deepest desires:

- To spend more quality time with my family.
- To write and shoot movies—something I had wanted to do since childhood.

- To create a soundtrack music album while being a stay-at-home dad.
- To have the time and freedom to be a part of causes bigger than myself.
- To experience the freedom of completely resetting the direction of my life.

Sure, I knew there were risks involved in following my dreams, but they were worth the *potential freedom* I could gain. After accepting that as fact, *I began to find it more comfortable to take the risk of freedom over the predictability of my paycheck.* It made more sense for me to risk it than to play it safe and be "set for life."

I realized that I was taking a risk either way. I just chose risks of adventure over the risks of a predictable, unchallenging life. It was incredible just how energizing choosing my own direction was.

There were monetary rewards, too. We've been able to invest in a lot of different things; to start, operate and sell businesses; to vacation all over the world; to pay off everything we owed and live debt-free for years.

My wife and I have also learned to simplify our lives and live off of less than we earn, to get rid of unnecessary accumulated "stuff"—yet to *enjoy more of life* than those who never take the chance to see the other side of risk for what it is: **open-ended opportunity**.

Redesign Your Life

We are all passionate about something. We just need to make an intentional decision to follow our dreams—to take a step out and allow ourselves to be vulnerable. The first steps of risk-taking will most likely be frustrating and discouraging, but the prize comes only to those who persevere.

The reason you have read this far is because you are different. You want the freedom of living without always having a cloud of debt hanging over your head. You want to be able to live life on your terms.

People like you, who choose to pursue more in life, make an intentional shift in their thinking. They make a conscious decision to reinvent themselves and exchange a little calculated risk for a taste of their dreams. To get back to the passion you once had about life, you need first to recall what made you feel so alive.

At one time you were passionate about being a singer or a cellist, an athlete or an actor, a model ship maker or a magician. It was your identity; it was who everyone knew you to be. Somewhere along the way, people with good intentions probably dissuaded you from pursuing your dreams, or you tried your craft in the real world and failed. You gave up without ever giving all that you knew you had inside to give.

Some people hold on to less-than-fulfilling careers for years solely out of fear of losing the *sense of security* that a job may or may not actually provide them. They pass on opportunity after opportunity whenever they smell any signs of risk. These people like knowing that the $2,428 will be deposited in their bank account on the 1st of this month at 9 a.m. sharp, just as it was last month and the month before that.

The problem is that the world we live in is no longer so predictable. Most people go through several career changes over their lifetime. Real job security is often no more than a distracting myth.

But you are no longer like them. You understand that life is to be lived and experienced to the fullest.

I'm giving you permission to explore your passions once again. Go out and buy a few magazines on mountain climbing or painting. Go to the rock concert and pay for the VIP all-access pass. Take an introductory flying lesson. Dare to touch your dreams again—no matter how much time has passed. They have been put deep inside of you for a reason. They are a significant part of who you are at your core; defying your dreams only leads to frustration.

Do you want to design remote-control model airplanes, take photos of national parks with an antique large-format camera, homeschool your son or daughter, be a nature guide in the Everglades, teach English in Beijing? What is stopping you?

Hint: It isn't your boss, your husband or wife, your parents, your credit card company, your past or even your present.

The truth is: *You* are stopping *you*.

Once I realized this hard fact, my life opened up and opportunities presented themselves to me. *Observe the world around you* and begin finding opportunities. No matter where you are in life, you can make the decision to **REDESIGN your life, starting now**. Take one step at a time.

Make the decision today to design what you really want your life to look like next month, in six months and a year from now.

Now you are asking: So what does following my dream and living my passions look like in the real world? What is the first step?

Get Paid to Dream: Do What You Love *as a Business*

To get paid to dream, you first need to define what your dream is. What would a day in the life of living your dream look like? What would it feel like?

What if I told you that you could live your passions once again and get paid for living your dream?

Here are some ideas as to how you can incorporate elements of living your dream while getting paid for it:

- **"I always wanted to be a rock star."** Begin by teaching students how to play piano or guitar and record musicians performing live. Get together with friends and plan a date when you will perform for an audience or at an open mic. Write and record a few songs of your own.
- **"I was so good at ballet in high school. I'd love to do that again."** Take a class at a local dance studio. Get back into your groove. Ask

to substitute or assistant teach. Start teaching a class on your own. Write up a curriculum (or reuse your curriculum from years ago). Get together with a friend who is good with a video camera and make a training video. Sell it online and get feedback from users, and then make another DVD incorporating that feedback.

- **"I want to make movies."** Start by videotaping weddings of friends and relatives. If you are more experienced, create training videos for local businesses. Write a short script and post a casting call for (unpaid) actors. Call upon the small businesses you worked with and have them sponsor your film. No excuses—make your movie!

- **"I've always wanted to be an artist."** Create commissioned artwork for organizations, or become a graphic designer and start a joint venture with web designers. Create your own fine-art pieces and rent gallery space for a weekend show, or approach small coffeehouses about showing your work.

- **"I've always wanted to write a book."** Learn how to write what people will pay for, like quality content for websites, brochures and advertisements. Start a joint venture with people who have the content for a book but are afraid to write it themselves. Offer to ghostwrite their book. While you are getting paid, write your book too!

- **"I think it would be great to be a stay-at-home parent."** Become an *Entrepreneurial Community Executive*. If you or your significant other wants to work full- or part-time, encourage him or her to do so. Run the property with the systems you have set up. Take a little time every day to work on your business venture. Spend time with your kids going on day trips and maybe even schooling them yourself.

- **"I love volleyball. I was captain of the team in college until my injury."** See if you can assistant coach a local team. Offer private or small group training. Teach all of the tricks you learned when you were in full swing. Teach principles of winning, diet and fitness. Students who have a desire to get a scholarship have parents who will support their getting additional training. Start-up costs for this are super-low. Play ball!

These are only a few ideas. Do you know what you would do with all of the money you aren't spending on your housing payments? What about the time that you will not be working at a full-time job? In reality, becoming a resident manager and running it as a Community Executive has enabled me to pursue several of these entrepreneurial endeavors, not just one.

Living outside of your purpose in life and setting aside your dream for some nebulous time in the future will leave you feeling unfulfilled. The purpose of life will rarely be found in an undemanding daily existence. We must continue to grow and improve ourselves daily—because like every other living thing on planet Earth, if we're not growing, we are dying.

So what about you? What will be your next move? I want to challenge you to bring to mind what it was that you were once so passionate about. What will inspire you enough to pick up that old dusty dream, clean it off and give it another chance? You will be surprised at the pleasure and vitality you will enjoy when pursuing your dreams. Unexpected doors will open when you determine to reset and redesign the pattern and direction of your future life.

ACTION PLAN

Chapter 17

THE SIMPLE 7-STEP GAME PLAN: HOW TO BE DEBT FREE, BUILD YOUR NEST EGG & LIVE LIFE ON YOUR OWN TERMS

This isn't just a book about real estate. For me to just write the how-to's but not help you with the bigger picture would be a disservice to you. When Fiona and I started out, we weren't just broke—we were *less than broke*. We were newlyweds with $38,000 in past-due credit card debt and no jobs to speak of. Credit collectors were calling us multiple times a day demanding payment. That was our starting point.

What we did have was the drive and a plan to get it together and get out of our financial situation as fast as possible. Below I have laid out the game plan Fiona and I used to get out of debt, get into investing into real estate and **pay off all of our debts** as quickly as possible.

Live Life On Your Own Terms   7. Return to Your Dream

_____   6. Go from Full to Part-Time

      Build a Nest Egg   5. Start Buying or Creating Assets

_____   4. Start a Simple Business You Enjoy

                        3. Redirect Money to Pay Off All Debt

  Become Debt Free   2. Pay Nothing for Your Home

_____ 1. Discipline Yourself to Live On Less

Step 1: Discipline yourself to live on less for a little while. Learn to deny yourself the shiny widgets. The car you drive now will probably keep going for another year or two. You have enough jewelry to accessorize your wardrobe for any occasion. Frugality is the key at this juncture. Ditching the TV and limiting Internet usage will yield you days of productivity every month. We haven't had cable or Internet service at home for almost a year now, and it is fantastic!

Step 2: Pay nothing for your home. Land a resident manager position. Having no housing costs will accelerate exponentially every financial move that follows. That is why I've spent much of this book showing you how Fiona and I have done this over these nine years and how we continue to do it. Once you do not have an $800-to-$2,500 monthly bite taken out of your paycheck for your rent or mortgage, it is like getting an enormous raise. For many it can be a 40 to 50 percent pay raise. Your spending power is multiplied by not having to pay for your largest expense month after month, year after year.

If you haven't done this already, do this little exercise right now:

Monthly housing cost $_____ x 12 months = **Instant** $_____ yearly raise

---

Step 3: Redirect the money previously spent on housing toward paying off ALL your debt. If you have been paying off debt you've accumulated over the years slowly, or you have only been getting deeper and deeper into debt every month, you can now see light at the end of the tunnel—and this time it isn't a train heading for you.

By simply using the income that was once allocated to paying your rent or mortgage and redirecting it toward your unsecured debt (credit cards, car loans, student loans, home equity loans, etc.), you will **decimate debt at twice the speed**. *That includes your small business debt.* Work to pay *any* outstanding debt attached to your name.

Step 4: Start a simple home-based business doing something you actually enjoy. What are you good at? What do you enjoy doing? What did you do at a previous job that you could do again as a consultant? You don't have to drop a million dollars and open a Wendy's to say you're a business owner. You don't have to make big profits, either. There are simply guidelines you must follow to be considered a legitimate business.

Contrary to popular belief, tax deductions are not loopholes. Loopholes are what the naive call knowledge of tax law. Tax deductions are one of the ways the government says, we approve of this, it is good for our economy, do more of it.

I'm not going to go through selecting and setting up a home-based business *in this book*. I am merely showing you that you don't have to be some pinstriped-suit-wearing, MBA genius to start photographing weddings on weekends for $500 to $1,500 a pop, make a few websites using WordPress for small businesses or become an online affiliate marketer.

Be sure to choose something that is a very low investment of *money as well as time*. You're not looking to lay out several thousand dollars on a hobby and make your life busier; you're looking to start learning how to run a business.

Having a home-based business also allows for amazing tax deductions that will help you keep more of your W-2/employee paycheck, as well. Contrary to popular belief, tax deductions are not *loopholes. Loopholes* are what the naive call knowledge of *tax law.* Tax deductions are one of the ways the government says, *We approve of this. It is good for our economy. Do more of it.*

Also, wrapping your business in a registered **entity** such as an LLC can give you and your assets protections that an **individual** does not have. That is what the wealthy do, and you can do it just as easily. You just need to know where to begin.

More about tax strategies for entrepreneurs are at www.CommExAcademy.com/lesstax.

Step 5: Start buying or creating real assets that will generate monthly income. In his book *Rich Dad Poor Dad, What the Rich Teach Their Kids About Money That the Poor and Middle Class Do Not!*, Robert Kiyosaki defines assets as things you own that put money *into your bank account*.

So that would not include your $5,000 engagement ring, your flat-panel TV or your new Dodge Charger with the 19-inch chrome rims. Also, your owner-occupied home is probably your biggest liability and *not* an asset, because it is the single biggest drain on your bank account. Owning a rental property, on the other hand, is an asset, since your renters pay down your mortgage, interest, property taxes and repairs when you structure things correctly.

If you own a house now, you can become a resident manager, move out of your house and rent it out. You keep the house, so you can move back to it someday if you want. In the meantime, have other people paying the mortgage and taxes for you. That is exactly what Fiona and I did.

Step 6: Go from full-time to part-time with your job. Once your income from your investments matches your income from your job and you have at least three months of living expenses in savings, you can decrease your job hours to what seems more comfortable for you.

You may love your job and wish to never leave it or think that this step is easier said than done. Or it may be difficult in your case to cut down hours without losing your job completely. You may, however, be surprised as to how you can begin working more of your work hours out of your home. At the very least, explore this option.

Step 7: Return to your dream—take time to do what you love.

Once you have decreased the hours you dedicate each week to your job, you need to fill it with something. Do you want to record an album, make a movie, train for an Ironman triathlon, create your own line of organic perfumes or volunteer more of your time at your favorite nonprofit? Now is your chance. Open up your horizons and finally begin to **live life on your terms**!

By now I hope you realize that the end goal isn't necessarily to be a resident manager or a Community Executive at the same property for the rest of your life. The big picture is to use the position to propel you into getting what you truly want out of life and to finally live life on your own terms faster than most people you will meet. In a short time, you will become more independent and will live debt-free, with the security that comes from having enough cash in the bank for any need, whim or adventure you wish to partake of. Enjoy the journey!

Congratulations!

One thing I know about you is that you're serious about taking control of your financial future.

I want to congratulate and reward you by offering a FREE MultiMedia Access Pass.

You will have special access to...

- ✔ The CE Quick Start Guide
- ✔ Easy-to-Follow Training Videos
- ✔ Welcome Video
- ✔ Unreleased Bonus Chapters
- ✔ Interviews

Take The Next Step

YOUR MULTIMEDIA ACCESS PASS

www.commexacademy.com/quickstart

Please Visit our website
www.CommExAcademy.com

- Find Additional information about our Community Executive Academy courses
  - **Online Courses** - Learn At Your Own Pace At Home
  - **Community Executive Certification Program**
  - **3-Day Community Executive Academy Intensive** - Live In Major Cities
  - **Property Management Team Training & Workshops**
  - **Landlord Training & Workshops**
- Get Your Questions Answered In Our Knowledgebase
- Find Out About Upcoming Events and Appearances

Contact Us:

Mail: Community Executive Academy
213 West Beltline Highway
Suite 101
Madison, WI
USA

Phone: (608) 554-0043

Fax: (866) 292-1527

E-Mail: info@commexacademy.com

Visit our website: www.CommExAcademy.com

ABOUT THE AUTHOR

Matthew & Fiona Peters are speakers, trainers and co-founders of the Community Executive Academy. Since 2001, they have developed & perfected "The Better-Than-Free Home™" lifestyle, which has given them the ability to acquire real estate, live mortgage free, eliminate their debts, build their nest egg, work less, and travel the world.

Matthew is a musician, award-winning videographer and principal of a multi-media company for the last 20 years. Fiona has owned and operated a property management company since 2001. They live in Madison, WI with their two toddlers Aidian and Kaiya.

BUY A SHARE OF THE FUTURE IN YOUR COMMUNITY

These certificates make great holiday, graduation and birthday gifts that can be personalized with the recipient's name. The cost of one S.H.A.R.E. or one square foot is $54.17. The personalized certificate is suitable for framing and will state the number of shares purchased and the amount of each share, as well as the recipient's name. The home that you participate in "building" will last for many years and will continue to grow in value.

Here is a sample SHARE certificate:

HABITAT FOR HUMANITY

THIS CERTIFIES THAT
YOUR NAME HERE
HAS INVESTED IN A HOME FOR A DESERVING FAMILY

1985-2005
TWENTY YEARS OF BUILDING FUTURES IN OUR
COMMUNITY ONE HOME AT A TIME

1200 SQUARE FOOT HOUSE @ $65,000 = $54.17 PER SQUARE FOOT
This certificate represents a tax deductible donation. It has no cash value.

YES, I WOULD LIKE TO HELP!

I support the work that Habitat for Humanity does and I want to be part of the excitement! As a donor, I will receive periodic updates on your construction activities but, more importantly, I know my gift will help a family in our community realize the dream of homeownership. **I would like to SHARE in your efforts against substandard housing in my community!** *(Please print below)*

PLEASE SEND ME _____ SHARES at $54.17 EACH = $ $_____

In Honor Of: _____

Occasion: (Circle One)   HOLIDAY   BIRTHDAY   ANNIVERSARY

        OTHER: _____

Address of Recipient: _____

Gift From: _____   *Donor Address:* _____

Donor Email: _____

I AM ENCLOSING A CHECK FOR $ $_____ PAYABLE TO HABITAT FOR HUMANITY <u>OR</u> PLEASE CHARGE MY VISA OR MASTERCARD *(CIRCLE ONE)*

Card Number _____ Expiration Date: _____

Name as it appears on Credit Card _____ Charge Amount $ _____

Signature _____

Billing Address _____

Telephone # Day _____ Eve _____

PLEASE NOTE: Your contribution is tax-deductible to the fullest extent allowed by law.
Habitat for Humanity • P.O. Box 1443 • Newport News, VA 23601 • 757-596-5553
www.HelpHabitatforHumanity.org

CPSIA information can be obtained at www.ICGtesting.com

224246LV00006B/116/P